*Contemporary Psychoanalysis
and Masterworks of Art and Film*

CONTEMPORARY PSYCHOANALYSIS
and Masterworks of Art and Film

Harry Trosman, M.D.

NEW YORK UNIVERSITY PRESS

New York and London

NEW YORK UNIVERSITY PRESS
New York and London

Copyright © 1996 by New York University

All rights reserved

Library of Congress Cataloging-in-Publication Data
Trosman, Harry.
Contemporary psychoanalysis and masterworks of art and film /
Harry Trosman.
p.   cm.
Includes bibliographical references and index.
ISBN 0-8147-8210-8 (alk. paper)
1. Psychoanalysis and the arts—History—20th century.   I. Title.
NX180.P7T76   1996
700'.1'9—dc20   96-10113
CIP

New York University Press books are printed on acid-free paper, and
their binding materials are chosen for strength and durability.
Manufactured in the United States of America
10 9 8 7 6 5 4 3 2 1

For Mardi
Michael, David
Elizabeth, Larry
Seth and Rebecca

CONTENTS

[vii]

Contents

ILLUSTRATIONS

ACKNOWLEDGMENTS

I would like to thank *The Psychoanalytic Quarterly* for permission to include previously published material in chapter 1 of this book.

A number of people have been of great help to me in the preparation of this book. I would like to thank Robert Michels, M.D., for clarifying the distinction between psychoanalysis as a practice and psychoanalysis as a scholarly activity. I am also grateful to Francis Baudry, M.D., and Jeffrey McClough, who have read parts of this manuscript and made valued suggestions. The members of the Department of Art at the University of Chicago have given me a background in art history and adopted me as one of their own. Miriam Hansen has greatly enlarged my understanding of film. Genevieve Curley has made a solid contribution in typing the manuscript.

[xi]

INTRODUCTION

*When we refer to psychoanalysis today, a variety of activities are impli-*cated. There is, of course, the psychoanalysis of the clinical prac-titioner engaged in psychiatric and psychological treatment, a practice which is carried out in collaboration with an analysand. The purpose is to help in the amelioration of symptoms, character pathology, or developmental deficiencies. This institutionalized activity is carried out by a group of specialists who have under-gone a long period of training, consisting of a personal analysis, the treatment of psychoanalytic patients under supervision, di-dactic work, and ongoing practice. It is based on the writings of Sigmund Freud and other analysts who have made subsequent clinical, technical, and theoretical contributions. Currently, there are a number of schools of clinical psychoanalytic thought, such as the Kleinian, the object relations school, the school of self psy-chology, and others; they are derived from Freud's original con-cepts, have added particular emphases of their own, and have played a role in modifying practice. To a large extent, these schools, although differentiated, maintain a common core and make use of technical means as well as a conceptual scheme which cuts across many of the differentiations.

Another type of psychoanalysis is what has been designated as applied psychoanalysis. This second type is carried out by psychoanalytic scholars. For the most part, these scholars are not engaged in the clinical practice of psychoanalysis, but have relied largely on the writings of Freud and other clinical psychoanalysts, using the empirical findings and theoretical works of the psychoanalytic practitioners as a basis for their scholarly contributions. Since the work of the scholars is based essentially on material found in books and journals rather than direct experience with the psychoanalytic method, there is an inevitable time lag. It has been remarked that the work of the scholarly psychoanalysts is often a good twenty years behind the contributions of the clinical psychoanalysts (Robert Michels 1995, personal communication). Since direct experience in doing psychoanalysis is not available to the scholar, the opportunity to have "the text speak back to one," which is essential and directly available to the clinician through the ever-present analysand, is not part of the scholarly endeavor. Although it has been suggested that a text can provide feedback for an interpretation, that a tentative hypothesis can be confirmed or contradicted by further immersion in a work, the text lacks the discursive byplay provided by the living analysand (Spitz 1985).

The psychoanalytic clinician exposed to the work of the applied psychoanalyst often finds a level of explanation which is less than satisfying. For example, in trying to account for the attraction of certain films with painful themes which bring about discomfort and terror in a viewer, the scholar may refer to Freud's work on masochism and argue in favor of a death instinct as an explanation for the presence of masochism. An explanatory power is attached to a metapsychological concept which is largely irrelevant as far as empirical findings regarding masochism are concerned. In addition to invoking highly abstract explanations, clinical formulations which have not stood the test of time may be invoked to account for the appeal of a work of art when such is no longer warranted. Appeal may be made to the use of energic concepts, overemphasis of libidinal themes, universal penis envy as a basis for feminine identity formation, and explanations of repression as a derivative product of anxiety. A great deal of attention may be paid to visualization as a genderized activity; as in the view that the male gaze directed toward a female is primarily a means of experiencing or discounting castration anxiety rather than the expression of an object interest. An interest in pornography may be understood as an expression of male power directed toward a depreciated female rather than as a perverse instinctualization meant to bolster an emptied and fragmenting self.

There is much of value that the applied psychoanalytic critic of art can find in the work of the psychoanalyst immersed in clinical practice. Although it is clear that the Freudian legacy still is bedrock and much of Freud's contribution is the mainstay of continuing practice, the last decades have added emphases in directions not found in Freud's original work.

I raise the distinction between the two types of psychoanalysis not to disparage the work of the psychoanalytic scholar nor to elevate the contribution of the psychoanalytic clinician. There are many psychoanalytic clinicians who are excellent practitioners, are helpful to their patients, and have a "clinical sense," but their work is limited to praxis and their contribution to psychoanalysis as an advancing discipline is minor; their contribution is constrained by the consuming demands of doing therapy. In addition, there have been psychoanalytic scholars who, despite lack of clinical experience, make outstanding contributions to their own disciplines. In literature, one thinks of Lionel Trilling, Kenneth Burke, Simon Lesser, Norman Holland, and Meredith Skura. Among art historians, one notes the contribution of Jack Spector, Meyer Schapiro, and Leo Steinberg; in film studies,

Laura Mulvey, E. Ann Kaplan, and Mary Ann Doanne deserve to be acknowledged.

In recent years and in response to the changing attitudes and shifts in institutionalized practice, more and more individuals who have not emerged from the mental health field have obtained direct clinical psychoanalytic exposure, thus enhancing their previous scholarship with new experience. Among those who have combined a clinical experience with applied work are Robert Waelder, George Devereux, Erik Erikkson, Ernst Kris, and in the current generation, Gilbert Rose, Glen Gabbard, Harvey Greenberg, Laurie Adams, and Gail Reed. As institutionalized psychoanalysis becomes liberated from its exclusionary constraints, one can assume that more and more scholars interested in the application of analysis will turn to clinical training as an appropriate means for immersing themselves in the psychoanalytic method.

As we consider psychoanalytic clinical work today, we are struck with several shifts in emphasis. Among the foremost of such changes has been the development of the notion of the psychoanalytic situation as an interactive field. The analyst is no longer considered to be an objective observer who is looking through a microscope at a field from which he is excluded. In fact, the analyst is considered to be part of the total field, and his position and responses during the course of the psychoanalytic session are given a value which heretofore was disregarded. What generally has been described as countertransference in its most generic sense is now considered to be an essential aspect of the psychoanalytic interaction. How the analysand affects the analyst in terms of emotional responses, fantasies, verbalizations, behavior, and other interventions are considered to be critical, and the analyst is inclined to accept his own responses as a continuing source of information in the exploration of the patient's intrapsychic reality. The psychoanalytic situation can be characterized as a realm of interactive subjectivities.

In addition, contemporary psychoanalysis is far less interested in reestablishing within consciousness the presence of a previously repressed memory, and is much more inclined to consider the analytic task in terms of establishing a coherent narrative. The distinction between historical and material truth, on the one hand, and narrative truth on the other, has moved in the direction of exposing and clarifying the personal myth as a valid therapeutic goal. To this extent, clinical practice has been affected by currents in the field of literature and the arts. The coherence of a narrative account has become a testable paradigm and, as enacted within the context of the transference situation, subject to examination and confirmation. A third contribution of contemporary psychoanalysis resides in the heightened importance attached to the central position of fantasy. It has become generally accepted that the intrapsychic elaboration of early experience in the form of unconscious fantasy plays a critical role in molding development and bringing about changes in the personality. Fantasy is regarded not only as the source of psychopathology but also as an important modality for the development of higher ego functions such as creativity and mastery. Here again, there is an close link established with the field of the arts.

The last few decades have seen a shift from an interest in instinct and drive to an interest in the field of object relations. The influence of Melanie Klein, W. Ronald D. Fairbairn, D. W. Winnicott, Heinz Kohut, and Otto Kernberg has heightened the view that psychic reality is largely dependent on modes of object relating. Whether we speak of the relation of self to internal object or one internal object to another, it is clear that early objects are laid down as anlage for the development of object relations later in life. The psychoanalytic situation provides an opportunity for the externalization of such object relations in the transference, and serves as a context in which such relationships can be clarified and understood.

Along with an interest in object relations, there has been an interest in attachment, separation, and individuation. This has been reflected in the importance that has been attributed to object loss, patterns of identification which develop as a result of such loss, and methods of compensation and substitution which compensate for shifts in object and attachments. Thus, modes of object relations have tended to supplement sexuality as an issue in psychoanalytic observation, and sexuality itself has been seen as one form of object choice which carries its own specific anxieties and modes of finding fulfillment. Here the original Freudian paradigm has been given a place within a wider context.

For the American psychoanalytic practitioner, the position of Jacques Lacan and his contribution is an interesting one. His work is accepted by some members of the second group—the psychoanalytic scholars—as being of great value, and his work on the imaginary and symbolic stages has been seen as useful in the understanding of certain aspects of art and film. Yet his work has played very little role in clinical practice in the United States, Canada, or the United Kingdom. The emphasis he has attached to language and the gaze has been used by literary and film critics as a valued contribution, while practitioners have found these notions either incorporated in the views of other object relations theorists or presented in such an obscure fashion that they do little to enhance the clinical situation. To some extent, Lacan has played a role in contemporary psychoanalysis similar to the position played by Carl Gustav Jung in a previous generation. He has served to provide a mode of access for psychoanalytic findings within a critical framework without disturbing the balance in favor of the primacy and inviolate status of the art work. Thus, the psychoanalysis of the clinician has been subverted partially by an emphasis on the art object and language and the mediating forms by which unconscious content is expressed.

To some extent, the psychoanalytic literature on art and film of the last two decades has tried to keep pace with the advances of psychoanalysis as a discipline. Jack Spector's 1988 article, "The State of Psychoanalytic Research in Art History," in the *Art Bulletin*, written by a nonclinician, is an extensive summary of prior psychoanalytic work and is informed by ongoing developments in depth psychology. The recent book by Laurie Adams (1993) is closely attuned to attachment theory and object relation psychology, and also takes into account shifts in current clinical practice. Ellen Handler Spitz, in *Art and Psyche* (1985), *Image and Insight* (1991), and *Museums of the Mind: Magritte's Labyrinth and Other Essays in the Arts* (1994), displays a sensitive awareness of the importance of object loss and compensatory reactions, particularly in her analysis of René Magritte's paintings. Gilbert J. Rose (1980, 1987) has been attuned to the importance of Mahlerian concepts regarding separation and individuation, rapprochement, fusion, and symbiosis as aspects of the formal relationships present in abstract painting.

When we turn to psychoanalytic approaches to film theory, Krin and Glen Gabbard in *Psychiatry and the Cinema* (1987) describe the representation of the psychiatrist and the psychoanalyst in films; they also offer a psychoanalytic understanding of the effects of films on the viewer and the psychological basis for their appeal. The volume edited by E. Ann Kaplan, *Psychoanalysis and Cinema* (1990), emphasizes a feminist approach to psychoanalytic film theory and is heavily influenced by Laura Mulvey's classical article, "Visual Pleasure and Narrative Cinema," originally written in 1973 and reprinted in her book *Visual and Other Pleasures* (1989). Kaplan includes in her volume Mulvey's second thoughts on the importance of the gaze, amending her previous notion that much of film could be understood in terms of a masculine gaze which finds woman as an anxiety-evoking, castrated object. Mulvey goes on to point out that women who find pleasure in cinema in part do so either by masochistic identifications or by a bisexual identification with the male. Much psychoanalytic film criticism, such as Christian Metz's *The Imaginary Signifier: Psychoanalysis and the Cinema* (1982), is heavily influenced by semiotics and Lacan. As mentioned above, in many ways this approach has seemed less useful than that of the Gabbards and Harvey R. Greenberg (1993), which views a selected number of Hollywood films through a contemporary psychoanalytic framework.

It is my conviction that the experience of the clinician adds an important dimension to the work of the psychoanalytic scholar who arrives at psychoanalysis through intellectual discourse. In the chapters that follow, I have applied the method of the clinician to the analysis of particular works of art, whether painting or film. In the works under discussion, I have considered them from the points of view of the presence of the observer in an interactive context, the generic family as an early object relation, lines of narration, attachment and separation, and the presence of fantasy as a factor in the development of a sense of reality and creativity. The masterworks presented can be approached profitably with such current insights and indeed have been chosen because they prompt an approach consonant with current psychoanalytic concerns.

In my description of Act I, Scene 1 of Shakespeare's *Hamlet* In *Freud and the Imaginative World* (Trosman 1985), I offered an example of an analysis which resembles that of the clinician as a participant in a psychoanalytic session. I demonstrated that aesthetic experience could be understood in terms of increase and decrease in shifting tension states when transmitted by formal and technical devices. My conceptual scheme was derived from Freud's *The Interpretation of Dreams* (1900). The method depended on the communicative effect of the components of the dream work, the particular mechanisms used by the dreamer in disguising the latent meaning by presenting a product structured by primary process ideation and characterized by formal techniques such as condensation, displacement, and substitution.

In this book, the method—enhanced by contemporary psychoanalytic perspectives—is applied to the analysis of particular works of visual art, such as painting and film. The interrelationship between stylistic innovation and critical life experience is further explored. In my examination of the precursors for the development of a contemporary psychoanalytic iconography in chapter 1, I note that Freud examined the interaction between critical psychological conflicts in the life of a creative artist and the impact on content in a subsequent work. Although Freud did not sufficiently emphasize Leonardo da Vinci's marked contribution to high Renaissance stylistic innovations—such as centralization and the pyramidal structure—formal artistic contributions could be understood psychologically as a product of internalized representations of family structure.

In subsequent chapters, I have chosen a number of works of art which are enigmatic in nature and thus evocative of a current analytic approach. Diego Rodriguez Velázquez's painting *Las Meninas* reflects the complex understanding current psychoanalysis takes toward the relationship between external reality, subjectivity, and the point of view of the observer. Analytic views of the analyst's point of view, the emotional response of the analyst to his patient, countertransference, the relationship between self and other, and the position of the observer within the psychological field, add new dimensions to our understanding of this work.

Giorgione's early sixteenth-century painting *The Tempest* is examined from the point of view of the primal familial relationship and the pastoral myth. Various aspects of the painting—such as the manner of lighting, the utilization of structural bridges, and the maintenance of distance and connectedness—are understood in terms of early forms of object relations, particularly of establishing connectedness between child and parental figures.

Georges Seurat's painting *Un Dimanche à la Grande Jatte* explores the theme of harmony and integration in the face of intrapsychic disunity and fragmentation. The formal relationship between the surface and depth of the painting establishes a unified configuration for social and interpersonal organization and tendencies toward fragmentation of individual figures and their activities. In the case of Seurat, recently discovered biographical information about his relationships with friends and family clarify a link between personality attributes—such as attachment and distance—and themes in the work.

Two Rembrandt van Rijn self-portraits, one in the Frick Museum, New York, and the other in Kenwood House, London, are used to demonstrate that aspects of biography are expressed through shifts in the relation between figure and background by means of light and spatial configurations. An analysis of the means of representation reveals how shifts in Rembrandt's fortune lead to the presentation of a self beset by adversity while striving for a sense of mastery enhanced by developing ego functions.

In addition to the analysis of particular works of painting, I also explore acknowledged masterpieces of film from the point of view of themes that are evocative of current psychoanalytic understanding. Michelangelo Antonioni's 1959 film, *L'avventura*, presents the particular twentieth-century theme of finding and maintaining object love in the face of narcissistic trauma and psychological emptiness. The film explores how a number of unfulfilled individuals use casual sexuality and noncommitment as compensatory devices in the face of object loss. The psychological experience of emotional emptiness is demonstrated by a formal analysis of space and configuration in the film.

The theme of object loss is also explored in the film by Orson Welles, *Citizen Kane* (1940–1941), an example of the link between narcissistic vulnerability and oedipal trauma. *Citizen Kane* and

L'avventura make their points aesthetically through the utilization of a frame of an investigation and a search. Explicitly in *Citizen Kane* the search is directed toward understanding the protagonist, and the search itself becomes a judgment of the psychoanalytic approach and its emphasis on historical and intrapsychic continuity. I demonstrate how, through technical devices, the viewer is implicated in the narrative of the film.

Alfred Hitchcock's *Vertigo* explores the role of fantasy in symptomatology and therapeutic interaction. Fantasy is demonstrated to be an integral component in the creation of reality testing. *Vertigo* highlights the vital importance of immersion in fantasy as a means of achieving psychological integration and conflict resolution. Federico Fellini's *8½* furthers the exploration of the utilization of fantasy—here as a necessary component in artistic creativity. The film demonstrates the steps in the disinhibition of creativity through a process of working through and the acceptance of regressive autobiographical insights as a result of endopsychic perception. The film demonstrates the necessity of achieving an acceptance of the blend of fantasy and reality testing in order to overcome the inhibitory factors in creativity.

In producing a work of art, a creator calls upon diverse aspects of an artistic personality, which are given cohesion and unity in the formation of the work itself. A masterpiece is the result of a significant synthesis in the life of a creator, during a period favorable for the integration of the component parts of intrapsychic reality and experience. The particular works of art examined demonstrate how such movements toward integration are discernible in the work.

REFERENCES

Adams, L. 1993. *Art and Psychoanalysis.* New York: IconEditions.
Freud, S. 1900. *The Interpretation of Dreams. Standard Edition.* Vols. 4 and 5. London: Hogarth Press.

Gabbard, K., and G. O. Gabbard. 1987. *Psychiatry and the Cinema*. Chicago: University of Chicago Press.

Greenberg, H. R. 1993. *Screen Memories: Hollywood Cinema on the Psychoanalytic Couch*. New York: Columbia University Press.

Kaplan, E. A., ed. 1990. *Psychoanalysis and Cinema*. New York: Routledge.

Metz, C. 1982. *The Imaginary Signifier: Psychoanalysis and the Cinema*. Bloomington: Indiana University Press.

Michels, R. 1995. The APA's psychoanalysis and the MLA's psychoanalysis: Differences and parallels. Unpublished address at the University of Chicago, March 14, 1995.

Mulvey, L. 1989. *Visual and Other Pleasures*. Bloomington: Indiana University Press.

Rose, G. J. 1980. *The Power of Form: A Psychoanalytic Approach to Aesthetic Form*. New York: International Universities Press.

———. 1987. *Trauma and Mastery in Life and Art*. New Haven: Yale University Press.

Spector, J. 1972. *The Aesthetics of Freud*. New York: Praeger.

———. 1988. The state of psychoanalytic research in art history. *Art Bulletin* 70:49–76.

Spitz, E. H. 1985. *Art and Psyche: A Study in Psychoanalysis and Aesthetics*. New Haven: Yale University Press.

———. 1991. *Image and Insight: Essays in Psychoanalysis and the Arts*. New York: Columbia University Press.

———. 1994. *Museums of the Mind: Magritte's Labyrinth and Other Essays in the Arts*. New Haven: Yale University Press.

Trosman, H. 1985. *Freud and the Imaginative World*. Hillsdale, N.J.: The Analytic Press.

{ One }

TOWARD A

Psychoanalytic Iconography

I begin with an examination and evaluation of previous psychoanalytic contributions to the visual arts. By iconography I refer to the useful term proposed by Erwin Panofsky (1962) to differentiate the study of the subject matter and meaning present in a work of art from a concern with form and style. Although I do not wish to eliminate style as a source of psychoanalytic interest and have discussed style elsewhere (Trosman 1985), in this chapter I propose narrowing the field to more common types of psychoanalytic studies. When I refer to psychoanalytic iconography, my aim is to offer a mode of interpretation for specific works of art that rests on the understanding of psychoanalytic theory, method, and empirical findings which result from the use of the method. Today we may find it difficult to delimit and specify exactly what is "psychoanalytic" when we examine some critical approaches since psychoanalysis has become not only a theory, a method of investigation, and a body of knowledge but also a contemporary intellectual attitude which permeates our cultural life. Thus, some of the current contributions to criticism and historical studies are not even manifestly referred to as psychoanalytic by their authors (Posner 1982; Steinberg 1983; Heller 1984). However, I believe that they rest on psychoanalytic principles.

[13]

I shall begin by tracing the development of this field by concentrating on Freud's monograph on Leonardo da Vinci (1910), his paper on the *Moses* of Michelangelo (1914), and Ernst Kris's classical study on Messerschmidt ([1933] 1952). I shall then describe the principles which underlie psychoanalytic iconography, with reference to specific studies and works of art which illustrate the application and limitations of these principles.

THE DEVELOPMENT OF A PSYCHOANALYTIC ICONOGRAPHY

Any attempt to examine the psychoanalytic contribution to the visual arts begins with a discussion of Freud's monograph on Leonardo da Vinci (1910). In his study, Freud placed the emphasis on Leonardo's childhood memory as a nodal point for a discussion of the artist's personality. Screen memories were considered to be clinical psychoanalytic data par excellence, and had already established an ancestry of some ten years as a legitimate source for forming psychoanalytic inferences (S. Freud 1899). Works of art in their own right until this time had a less legitimate position as data in the psychoanalytic canon. Admittedly, several times prior to 1910, Freud had referred to works of art— such as *Oedipus Rex* or Jensen's *Gradiva* (S. Freud 1900, 1907)— but such references had been largely illustrative in support of a formulation which already was based on clinical grounds. Until the publication of the Leonardo da Vinci book, there had been no attempt to examine a work of art as a means for enlarging the understanding of the personality of the artist.

It should also be stated here that, even when Freud did examine works of art in the monograph on Leonardo, he did so primarily in order to make a biographical point. Thus, it is debatable whether Freud's references to the paintings of Leonardo were intended as a form of psychoanalytic criticism which adds understanding to the work itself independent of biographi-cal reflections. Freud made references to the paintings of the *Mona Lisa* (ill. 1.1), the *Madonna and Child with St. Anne* (ill. 1.2), *St. John the Baptist,* and the *Bacchus* in the context of describing a preoccupation in the mind of the artist. Freud thus opened up the problem of psychoanalytic art criticism by considering the work itself as an expression of the individual artist's preoccupa-tion.

In the intervening years, Freud's book on Leonardo da Vinci has been subjected to much critical evaluation (Maclagan 1923; Wohl and Trosman 1955; Schapiro 1956; Eissler 1961; Farrell 1963; Gombrich 1965; Wolheim 1970; Lichtenberg 1978). Almost every piece of evidence which Freud used in order to substantiate his view of Leonardo's personality has been called into question, either by further historical research or by subsequent psychoana-lytic findings. This being the case, one might well question what continues to be valuable in the book and what is a legitimate progeny for current research and further studies.

We recall that in his monograph Freud first presented the enigmatic quality of Leonardo's personality, pointing out that he was poorly understood by his own contemporaries; they did not understand why he could not finish his artistic works or concern himself with elevating his status as a true Renaissance artist should. Instead, he seemed to be desultory in his artistic interests and neglected them in favor of apparent trivialities, such as interests in experimental studies or naturalistic and scientific explorations of nature.

Freud reasoned that much of Leonardo's personality was ex-plicable in the analysis of a childhood memory of a vulture having opened his mouth with its tail and striking him many times against his lips while he was lying in the cradle. Building on the little that was known about Leonardo's childhood and his birth, including his illegitimacy, led Freud to reason that Leo-

1.1 Leonardo da Vinci, *Mona Lisa* (Paris: Louvre).

1.2 Leonardo da Vinci, *Madonna and Child with St. Anne* (Paris: Louvre).

nardo spent the initial period of his life in a close oedipal attachment with his mother, an abandoned peasant girl, before he was taken from her and admitted to the home of his newly married father. Thus, he was exposed to two maternal figures, his biological mother and a stepmother, who had no children of her own. Leonardo puzzled about sexual matters and had an early fantasy of parthenogenetic birth, endowing his mother with both masculine and feminine qualities. His intense oedipal involvement led to a preoccupation with sexual curiosity and inhibition as far as his overt sexual behavior was concerned, but he succeeded in sublimating his sexual interests in the direction of scientific curiosity and interest in nature. For many years, Leonardo found himself in constant conflict between his artistic and scientific interests; he pursued a course of commitment to science until sometime in his fifties, when he met La Gioconda, who reactivated the childhood memories of his abandoned mother, whose smile Mona Lisa shared. Leonardo became intensely immersed in painting the *Mona Lisa* in order to capture her personality and the fleeting nature of her smile. Subsequently, he developed an interest in depicting the two mothers of his childhood who then appear in the *Madonna and Child with St. Anne*. He continued an interest in depicting the smile and the androgynous nature of his mother in the later paintings of *St. John the Baptist* and the *Bacchus*.

In addition, Leonardo maintained an ambivalent relationship with his father, who had interfered with his intense mother attachment, and Leonardo was in conflict over the resultant hostile and aggressive feelings. He established a reactive identification with father surrogates, such as Ludovico Sforza, the Duke of Milan, and he shared with both his father and the duke the sense that he, like them, was unable to finish tasks that he had started. The accusation posterity brought against him he expressed about Sforza: "None of the works that he undertook was completed" (S. Freud 1910, 122).

As I stated previously, Freud in the Leonardo da Vinci book was primarily interested in the utilization of psychoanalysis for biographical purposes. Thus, the data that he used for his synthesis of Leonardo's personality was the meager data of historical documentation and the findings of about twelve years of clinical psychoanalytic work. He could use, of course, only the historical data that was available to him at the time, but since the writing of his original monograph, questions have been raised about both his psychoanalytic formulations and the historical evidence, in the light of new data.

As early as 1923 (Maclagan 1923), it had been pointed out that Freud had made a serious error in his description and utilization of Leonardo's early memory. The bird that Leonardo had referred to—"nibbio" in Italian—was not a vulture but a kite. Freud had erred in using a German translation from the Italian, by Maria Herzfeld, which had misidentified the bird. In spite of Freud's utilization of Italian in other places in the book and his apparent knowledge of the language, he did not check the Herzfeld translation. Doubtless out of his own wishes to support his thesis about the meaning of the vulture as both an Egyptian and a Medieval symbol of parthenogenetic impregnation, he was led astray. By not pursuing the psychoanalytic meaning associated with kites, about which Leonardo wrote in other contexts, Freud missed an important piece of evidence, which would have suggested an alternate view of Leonardo's relationship with his mother.

In addition, Freud, who was at the beginning of his investigation into psychogenetic antecedents for male homosexuality and had not yet had a wide experience with patients of this type, tended to overestimate one particular constellation, namely, overattachment to the mother and abandonment by the father, with a formation of a feminine identification as a result of the intense maternal attachment. Through subsequent years, alternate dynamic and genetic explanations have been offered for other types of homosexuality, and it is quite possible that such explanations—as for example, the situation which governed the early life of Michelangelo—might have applied equally well in Leonardo's case (Wohl and Trosman 1955; Liebert 1983).

Thirdly, Freud at the time of the writing of his book was unaware of an important piece of historical documentation which appeared in 1939 (Möller). A tax return of Leonardo's grandfather was discovered indicating that Leonardo was present in the home of his grandfather at birth, and the grandfather lists the names of the ten godparents who were present at the time of the baptism. Thus, it is likely that Leonardo was not abandoned at birth by his father nor shortly after his birth by his mother. In addition, subsequent work has called into doubt the whole issue of a conflict between a scientific and an artistic part to his personality, Leonardo's lack of interest in Christianity, and the orthodox views of religion of the time. Additional historical, social, and psychological meanings have been ascribed legitimately to the early memory. The smile in Leonardo's work has been further explicated as less than unique; the particular contribution Leonardo made to Renaissance art has been given a much more specific and precise description than the one that Freud offered (Schapiro 1956; Clark 1967).

We may well ask after such thorough criticism, what value can we continue to attribute to Freud's book and what is the legacy for the psychoanalytic iconographer who approaches the visual arts today? It is paradoxical that many of the art historians who have been critical of Freud's approach have at the same time praised the boldness of his contribution. None has suggested an alternate and equally encompassing view of Leonardo's personality. Many would agree with the general psychoanalytic view, that the work of art is a product of personality in depth, as long as this view is presented as a general statement. The art historical approach has been concerned primarily with seeing works in the context of an artistic tradition and has conceived the shaping of a work of art in terms of a rationalistic psychology dedicated to problem-solving and concern with formal problems. *Pari passu* there has been an interest in considering the work as expressive of the creator's personality. "That impulses from the depths of the psyche feed into works of art is not in doubt," states the art historian (Steinberg, 1984, 45), even when there is intense incredulity when confronted with specific psychodynamic and genetic formulations.

There are at least two fundamental principles which were proposed in the Leonardo da Vinci book and which continue to maintain a place in psychoanalytic art criticism to this day. First, Freud viewed an original art work in the context of a critical life experience in the life of the artist. His crucial example in the Leonardo book is the view that, since the *Mona Lisa* was a portrait from which Leonardo could not part—he kept the picture for the rest of his life—the meeting with this woman was a significant psychological experience in Leonardo's life, and this meaningful psychological experience affected the direction of his work. Here, Freud could point not only to the importance of both the sitter and the painting for Leonardo but also to the critical responses of the centuries, which suggest a shared universality in both the experiences and the responses. Freud provided an explanation for the importance that the ages have attached to this icon, an explanation derived from the emotional importance we attach to the early mother-child bond.

A second contribution of Freud's monograph is to suggest a psychological link with the issue of motif or iconographic imprint. Freud saw the *Madonna and Child with St. Anne*, the *Bacchus*, and the *St. John* as linked by the emotional attachment Leonardo established on the basis of an identification with androgynous figures who find in the narcissistic object an image of their own idealized selves. Freud's contribution was to provide an experiential basis for what might generally be called the artist's characteristic motif. The artist finds means for the satisfaction of fundamental drives through the manipulation of his artistic tools and the performance of his artistic task. When Schapiro (1956) emphasized a particular contribution of Leonardo to the art of the Renaissance, he did not emphasize the issue of smiles or the pyramidal form that Kris ([1933] 1952) attributed to Leonardo. Instead, regarding the *Madonna and Child with St. Anne,* Schapiro focused on the interlocking forms of the figures, and the attempt at an organic dynamic unity among the figures, which made familial relationships a theme for formal expression. One of the irrefutable facts in Leonardo's early life, namely his illegitimacy and possible marginality, makes such a concern understandable.

The critical response which met the Leonardo book did not follow the publication of Freud's paper on the *Moses* of Michelangelo (1914a). In fact, little attempt has been made to deal with this work, in either an art historical or psychoanalytic context. (Wollheim's 1970 paper is an exception to this neglect.) This is surprising in view of the fact that Freud in this paper subjects a work of art to a meticulous visual analysis, an approach which is by no means alien to the art historian. In addition, Freud deals here with a specific work of art, and uses the psychoanalytic method not for purposes of psychobiography but for purposes of illuminating the nature of the work itself.

The *Moses* paper clearly deserves careful attention. Freud begins by making a distinction between being moved by a work and not feeling a sense of satisfaction until he had had an opportunity to analyze the factors which were responsible for his emotional response. He supports the view that aesthetic response is motivated by unconscious factors, and he adds a dimension to the pleasure to be derived from critical understanding, a kind of after-pleasure in addition to the initial aesthetic resonance. He also suggests that we are moved essentially by something in the artist's intention, that the intention is present in the work, and that the artist strives to recreate in us, the viewers, an emotional attitude similar to his own in the process of creation.

Freud describes the intensity of his own response to the *Moses* statue (ill. 1.3) and his need to return to it time after time in order to puzzle out its strange effect upon him.

> No piece of statuary has ever made a stronger impression on me than this. How often have I mounted the steep steps from the unlovely Corso Cavour to the lonely piazza where the deserted church stands, and have essayed to support the angry scorn of the hero's glance! Sometimes I have crept cautiously out of the half-gloom of the interior as though I myself belonged to the mob upon whom his eye is turned—the mob which can hold fast no conviction, which has neither faith nor patience, and which rejoices when it has regained its illusory idols. (S. Freud 1914a, 213)

Freud points out that there has been a puzzle about the statue, centered around the issue of whether it was meant to be a depiction of a moment in the life of Moses or whether it was meant to be a study in character. He describes the varied critical responses; some critics have seen the statue as that of a wrathful Moses with pain and contempt on his face, who has just witnessed the people worshiping the Golden Calf following his descent from Mount Sinai with the Tables of the Ten Commandments under his arm. Others have pointed out that, since the *Moses* statue was meant to be part of a large commemorative tomb for Julius II and to be placed at a corner of the second story, it is unlikely that Moses was to be seen as about to rise up from the tomb in order to castigate the people; thus the positioning of the statue was meant to express a decorative effect.

1.3 Michelangelo, *Tomb of Pope Julius II,* detail of *Moses* (Rome: S. Pietro in Vincoli).

Applying the method of the psychoanalyst in paying careful attention to small details of the work—since "psychoanalysis is accustomed to divine secret and concealed things from despised or unnoticed features" (S. Freud 1914a, 222)—Freud noted two features of the statue which had been heretofore neglected. He noticed the attitude of the right hand and the position of the two Tables of the Law under the right arm. Freud observed that strands from the left side of Moses's beard were positioned so that they were on the right side of his body. Freud reasoned that what we see is a retreating motion of the right hand and that we are to imagine that, prior to the depiction of the statue, Moses had grasped the full beard with all the fingers of his right hand. What we see in the current statue is a retreating motion of the right hand after the beard is let go. Freud reasoned that Michelangelo was depicting a Moses who indeed has witnessed the people worshipping the Golden Calf as he paused in his descent from Mount Sinai, carrying the Tables under his right arm. His initial response is one of wrath, and he grasps his beard in order to rise and express the full measure of his indignation. In rising, however, he loosens his grasp on the Tables, and they are about to slip and break from under his arm. He then quickly releases his hand from the beard in order to control the precious Tablets and inhibit their destruction. In other words, he is tempted to take vengeance but rises above the temptation, and the whole sculpture becomes a "concrete expression of the highest mental achievement that is possible in a man, that of struggling successfully against an inward passion for the sake of a cause to which he has devoted himself" (S. Freud 1914a, 233).

In drawings, Freud illustrated what he assumed to be the previous positions of Moses which Michelangelo had in mind (ill. 1.4). In figure 1, Moses is presented sitting calmly; in figure 2, enraged as he notices the apostasy, he is about to jump to his

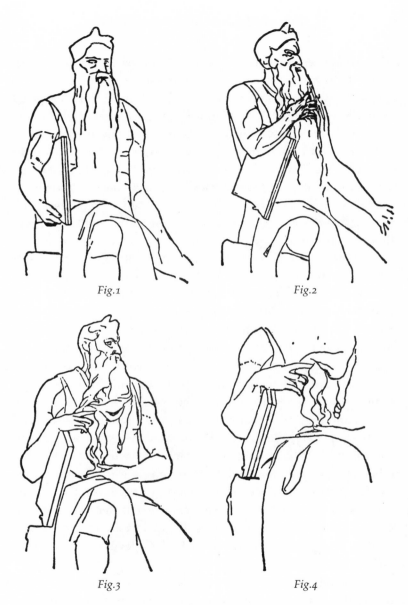

Fig.1   Fig.2

Fig.3   Fig.4

1.4 From *Collected Papers*, vol. 4, by Sigmund Freud. Authorized translation under the supervision of Joan Riviere. Published by Basic Books, Inc., 1959, by arrangement with The Hogarth Press Ltd. and The Institute of Psycho-Analysis, London. Reprinted by permission.

feet. Figures 3 and 4 display the figure as it actually exists, following the inhibition of the outburst.

Freud corrects the biblical view of Moses as having destroyed the Tables, pointing out that the biblical text is garbled and unlikely to be historically accurate. Freud also hazards a biographical interpretation suggesting that Michelangelo was depicting a reproach against Julius and himself—two men given to violent tempers and unrealistic grand schemes—thus expressing a premonition of the failures to which they were both doomed. However, the biographical reflection is mentioned only in passing. It is a minor point in a study concerned with the work per se.

Quite clearly, Freud sees the work of art as an expression of an underlying psychological reality. He identifies with those who "had emancipated themselves from the visual image of the statue" (S. Freud 1914a, 229) in order to understand something of the unconscious motives which lie behind it. In addition—and I believe this is crucial—Freud finds that after a thorough analysis of the manifest content of the statue, one arrives at a valid psychoanalytic principle, an expression of a psychological truth imbedded in the statue—namely, with progressive development, the taming and transformation of drive through the participation of ego influences lead to psychological growth and creativity (Trosman 1985).

Freud's interpretation of the Moses statue was directly related to a crisis in his own life. We have clear reference to the fact that as he wrote the paper Freud was responding to the apostasy of Jung and Adler from the psychoanalytic movement; his feelings toward the dissidents were those which he attributes to Moses as he notes the people worshipping the Golden Calf. Freud himself made reference to the similarities the two situations (Jones 1955, Letter of October 17, 1912, 367); he wrote the *Moses* paper shortly after his last attempts to reconcile Jung to his views of the libido theory; and in the same year, 1914, he expressed his feelings toward the dissidents in his polemical work "The History of the Psychoanalytic Movement" (S. Freud 1914b). We note the use of conscious subjectivity as a factor in the understanding of a work of art. We may hazard the inference that the aggressive energy freed and transmuted in reconciling Freud to the unavoidable defection served as a stimulus toward the creative insights of the Moses paper.

The methodological difficulty here, of course, is the problem of whether one has projected too much of one's own preoccupation into the work and thus has colored the meaning in terms of subjective need. Is Freud's interpretation referable to the statue or is it a distortion due to Freud's self-preoccupations? The question of evidence is to be answered by the thoroughness of the analysis and the fit between interpretation and elements of the work. Those who find fault with Freud's interpretation can justify their criticism by further examination of the manifest content and proposing alternate interpretations. For example, is it true that right hand is actually supporting the Tables under the armpit as Freud assumes? Does the manner of grasping the beard with the full hand denote reverence in the presence of God rather than the expression of anger turned against the self (Janson 1968)? Freud, sensitive to such criticism, responds that when considering a creator with the capacity for expressive thought such as Michelangelo, one can probably credit him with more intention rather than less. But finally, Freud is quite prepared to accept the idea that the artist himself may not succeed in creating in his work what he fully intended. On occasion, the psychoanalytic critic must fill in the artist's lack of success with a valid psychoanalytic interpretation accounting for failure as well as success.

One readily can understand why Freud's paper met with so little critical response. In an era devoted to respecting the sanctity of the manifest text, Freud's analysis seems arbitrary. Although he makes a careful analysis of small details of the statue itself, when it suits his purpose he gives up the detailed description and turns instead to an interpretation of intent which is at some remove from the direct description. In addition, the interpretation of intent itself cannot be documented by any historical evidence, such as letters or plans for the commission which would support Freud's point of view. Thus, Freud pleases neither the new critics nor the traditionalists, and seems to permit the potentiality for a wide range of interpretations independent of the work or a factual description of its historical context. In addition, is there universal agreement about the "highest mental achievement that is possible in a man, that of struggling successfully against an inward passion for the sake of a cause to which he has devoted himself"? As Shakespeare reminds us in *Henry V,* "what if the cause be not just?" Does the same hold?

Freud himself apparently had reacted to another view of the *Moses* statue earlier in his life—not as if it were an exemplar of a successful struggle against a violent passion but as an accusatory figure who shamed him as a member of a mob lacking conviction and faith, and wishing for illusory idols. Thus, we are left with continuing possibilities of multiple interpretations, and must turn instead to an example of a psychoanalytic view of art works in which their understanding seems fairly precise and certain. In making such a transition, we find that we are on safer ground if we can connect the work of art to a direct expression of what we know about psychopathology.

In psychoanalytic circles, it has been generally accepted that Ernst Kris's paper on Messerschmidt ([1933] 1952) represents a high point in the application of psychoanalytic knowledge to the understanding of particular works of art (Kohut 1960). Franz Xaver Messerschmidt (1736–1784) was a successful sculptor who lived in Vienna and initially worked in a late Baroque style for the Austrian aristocracy and the members of the Hapsburg court.

Prior to 1770, he did busts of the Emperor Josef II and Maria Theresa in a rhythmic, flowing style in keeping with the tradition of Bavarian and Austrian rococo. In the early 1770s, he developed a psychotic illness and felt that he was persecuted "by all of Germany." He was passed over for a professorship in the Academy of Vienna because he was considered unqualified to teach, and he left the capital to live in the provinces, where occasional visitors described him as "scurrilous, scornful, and isolated." At about this time, the style of his work changed. From the early 1770s on, he became preoccupied with doing a series of life-sized male busts—more than sixty were found in his studio after his death—which depicted a variety of human expressions. Messerschmidt strove to represent changes in the facial musculature, such as grimacing and smirking (ill. 1.5). He was not concerned with the expression of affects or with the expression of personality traits; the emphasis of the work was on facial distortions and muscular shifts such as yawning, clenching the teeth, and pressing the lips together.

The content of Messerschmidt's psychosis consisted of delusional and hallucinatory experiences. He believed himself to be tortured by demons who visited him at night and produced painful sensations in his lower abdomen and thighs. He engaged in a number of apotropaic mechanisms in order to ward off magically the intrusions of the disturbing demons. He would pinch himself repeatedly while looking in the mirror as he worked. He would clamp his lips together in order not to show the red of his lips because this stirred the demons, and he would repeatedly look at himself in the mirror while working. His florid psychosis—apparently a paranoid type of schizophrenia—although related to the stylistic changes in his work, did not interfere with the technical quality of his sculpture, which continued to be of a high order.

Kris, who was initially trained as an art historian, wrote his

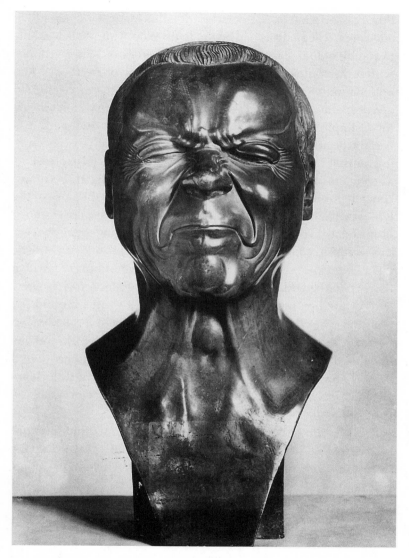

1.5 Franz Xaver Messerschmidt, *The Morose Man* (Vienna: Österreichische Galerie).

Ph.D. dissertation on Messerschmidt as his interest in and knowledge of psychoanalysis had begun to develop. Thus, Kris was able to combine dual careers and to view the work of Messerschmidt within the context of the psychoanalytic view of psychosis. Kris understood Messerschmidt's behavior as attempts at a restitution of a desperate attachment with a reality from which he felt himself to be slipping. As he doubted the existence of his own person, it became necessary to document his sense of being alive by examining himself repeatedly in the mirror for genuine facial expressions as a means of establishing a psychic identity. The busts became a concrete form of his new psychic reality. However, because of the hollowness and the disintegration in his affective responses, many of his busts expressed little in the way of genuine emotional expression, and concentrated instead on reflex reactions and autistic facial expressions. Among the latter are several busts in which there is marked distortion of the features of the face, such as pressure of the lips together and elongation of the area around the mouth as if to "shut out the demons." Kris noted a relationship between the constrained conciseness of his later work and the likelihood that his adoption of a neoclassical style tending toward formalism was well suited to the detached attitude of the schizophrenic, who feared the intrusion of disruptive emotional responses.

Kris was attracted to the study of a psychotic sculptor because in contrast with the work of someone normal or neurotic, the intrusions of the psychotic process were more likely to be apparent as obvious anomalies within the context of an established artistic tradition. If we can note aspects of the psychosis in the presence of the work of Messerschmidt, then it is likely that he is an extreme case of a principle which may be more generally valid. It may be likely that private meanings are attached to a variety of the aspects of an artist's work, including the formal elements for which he has a particular preference. In the case of

Messerschmidt, we note the intrusion of products of psychotic ideation: pressed lips avoid libidinal incorporation and demon possession. Thus, the work itself can be understood in terms which characterize a progression within a psychotic process.

Kris's study, thus, is more clearly related to Freud's early work on Leonardo da Vinci than his paper on the *Moses* statue. Just as Leonardo could depict his preoccupation with family ties and illegitimacy in the *Madonna and Child with St. Anne,* so Messerschmidt found through physiognomic studies an opportunity to express his need to deal with his psychosis. In Messerschmidt, the psychotic mechanisms influenced the content of his creativity and merged with the intact part of his personality. His character heads are to be understood in the context of intrapsychic activity. Insofar as Messerschmidt, late in his life, returned to portrait heads in the more conventional sense, he continued to manifest a fine skill as a portrait artist, and within a neoclassical style produced remarkable works in which remnants of his psychotic preoccupations continued to be only dimly present as an undercurrent. One such work, referred to as a portrait of a Capuchin monk, Fessler (ill. 1.6), also known as "a Dominican monk," depicts an expressive head characterized by the pinched lips Messerschmidt described as necessary in order to ward off the evil demons. In the portrait bust, however, the expression around the mouth is fully integrated, and does not detract from the totality of the aesthetic effect of the work. Thus, reactions stirred by a psychotic process may be adapted to tasks of artistic creativity and perhaps even serve as a stimulus to innovation and stylistic developments. What originally had been an excessive stylization secondary to psychotic stereotypy, may become integrated within a stylistic development and further artistic liberation. It may also be the case that such artistic liberation continues to play a part in the self-healing as an adaptive response to the psychotic process.

1.6 Franz Xaver Messerschmidt, *The Capuchin Monk* (Bratislava [Pressburg]: Stadtische Galerie).

PRINCIPLES OF A PSYCHOANALYTIC ICONOGRAPHY
AND ILLUSTRATIVE STUDIES

The integration of a psychoanalytic approach to works of art can be so seamless that we are occasionally left unclear about whether there is anything "psychoanalytic" about the critical approach at all. A study of Jean-Honoré Fragonard's painting *The Swing* (ill. 1.7) points out that the painting is a depiction of joyous sexuality (Posner 1982). The author states that "until very recently the mores of art historical criticism made it difficult to really think about" (82) the sexual meaning of the picture. The artist has depicted the rising tide of sexual passion in a naturalistic scene, which heightens the sense of excitement. A man in the background swings a young woman. As she reaches the crescendo of her swing, her lover extends his arm and his hat in a rigid position, pointing them between her parted legs as she kicks off her shoe to signal the culmination of her movement.

A number of additional components of the painting heighten the sexual theme—the private nature of the setting, the Cupid who urges silence, the act of swinging itself, and so forth. The apt synthesis of the ideational and the visual content of the symbols provides the basis for the aesthetic response. Posner, in his analysis of the painting, nowhere invokes psychoanalysis by name nor does he refer to Freud's discussion of the hat as a phallic symbol or the shoe as a feminine symbol, as in the *Introductory Lectures* (S. Freud 1916–1917). The implication is that Fragonard and his patron were fully aware of the sexual symbolism, but in the intervening two centuries, this awareness passed into "modern oblivion," to borrow a pertinent recent term (Steinberg 1983). Nineteenth-century viewers responded to the work on an unconscious level, finding justification for their pleasure in an appreciation of rococo style and the playfulness of the subject without acknowledging they were viewing a signified sexual union. The formal devices of the work provide an aes-

1.7 Jean-Honoré Fragonard, *The Swing* (London: Wallace Collection). Reproduced by permission of the Trustees of the Wallace Collection.

thetic distance, aiding disguise and thus allowing the unconscious content to find an acceptable mode of discharge. It should be noted that in this critical approach a psychoanalytic view of *The Swing* has little to do with the biographical importance of this particular painting in the life of the artist himself.

When we turn to a psychoanalytic approach to Edvard Munch (1863–1944), biographical factors are once more pertinent. Munch has long been a subject of psychoanalytic interest (Steinberg and Weiss 1954; Hodin 1956), and in some ways Munch's expressionist works are even more transparent of psychic content than Fragonard's. A frequent theme is that of a seductive woman who abandons herself to desire and is highly destructive toward men who are engulfed by her (ill. 1.8 and 1.9), or both men and women are hopeless pawns of a blind nature, which through sexuality guides their mutual fate to death and destruction. Recent scholarly works on Munch (Heller 1978a, 1978b; Stang 1979; Eggum 1984; Heller 1984) have provided the psychoanalytic investigator with an opportunity for the understanding of Munch's thematic preoccupation.

The Norwegian painter was born in 1863, the second child in a sibship of five. His mother, who married at the age of twenty, was twenty one years younger than her husband, and tubercular at the time of marriage. Edvard, the second child and first boy, was followed by three siblings in quick succession, and the mother died of tuberculosis when the boy was five, perhaps pregnant with her sixth child. The boy developed a close attachment to his sister, two years older, who also died of tuberculosis when he was fourteen. The mother at the time of her death left a poignant letter to the young boy, advising him to obey his strict father, who, following her death, became a religious fanatic and a model of moralistic rectitude. She wrote of her blissful wish to have the young boy join her in heaven following his death. Through his adolescence and early manhood, Munch maintained an intense ambivalent re-

1.8 Edvard Munch, *Madonna* (Chicago: The Art Institute of Chicago).
Courtesy of The Art Institute of Chicago.

1.9 Edvard Munch, *The Vampire* (Chicago: The Art Institute of Chicago). Courtesy of The Art Institute of Chicago.

lationship with his father, and allied himself with a Bohemian group in Oslo in defiance of paternal values.

A crucial work in Munch's career was the painting, *Night*, (ill. 1.10) of 1890 (Heller 1978b). The painting was a reaction to the news of the death of his father, and depicts a man sitting in a room, head bowed, preoccupied with mournful thoughts. It is painted in a symbolist style at variance with the naturalistic work Munch had been doing in the previous few years. Shortly following the death of Munch's father and the painting of *Night*, Munch experienced the most creative decade of his life, and did the body of work for which he is most highly regarded today. In 1907–1908, Munch experienced a psychiatric illness necessitating

1.10 Edvard Munch, *Night in St. Cloud* (Oslo: Nasjonalgalleriet). Photo: Jacques Lathion.

a period of hospitalization over several months, and his style then changed to that of a more decorative and less innovative and emotionally intense manner. In the last few decades of his life, he isolated himself from social contact, literally surrounded himself by his own work—which he saw as extensions of his own personality—tending to treat his paintings as if they were actual living beings, speaking of them as if they had personalities of their own.

Munch's preoccupation with the aggressive and destructive power of female sexuality was in reaction to his mother's early death following her series of pregnancies. In his view, his father had caused his mother's death by his sexual demands, sexuality itself was a destructive force which led to separation and death. The two most important losses in Munch's early life occurred when his libidinal energies were stirred, at the height of his oedipal phase and at the beginning of his adolescence. His mother's frequent pregnancies were seen as the result of his father's overwhelming and destructive sexual demands. Munch reversed the gender of the sexually aggressive partner in his work following the death of his father, in part as a means of handling his own ambivalence and propitiating his father, who was now seen as not responsible. The theme of the aggressive woman served as a cover for her powerlessness and victimization. It was no longer women who were engulfed, but men who had to defend themselves against women. Women threatened men by offering them a reunion through death.

In *Night*, Munch depicts himself as mourning the death of his father. He appears in the process of grieving, recalling the memories of his recently lost, ambivalently cathected father, and through these memories, recalling the death of his sister and his mother. The mourning experience reactivated the old losses, and it is the working-through of these recollections which then leads to a renewed phase of creativity and originality. As he often stated, "I paint not what I see but what I saw." In Munch's view, art thrives on death, and the creation of the work of art itself is an expression of an erotic transformation. The artist becomes truly androgynous by fertilizing himself; by using memories of his past experiences as seminal for inspiration, he becomes self-generating.

In sum, a review of current art historical studies, such as new views of Fragonard's *The Swing* and studies on Munch, enables the psychoanalyst to enlarge the scope of the early studies by Freud and Kris. In considering the use of psychoanalysis in such studies, we can consider the range and applicability of psychoanalysis in order to determinate general principles which underlie such studies.

The principles underlying a psychoanalytic approach concern themselves with: (1) the work of art as an expression of the biography of the artist; (2) the work of art as a representation of unconscious psychological content; (3) the aesthetic response to a work of art as a subject for psychoanalytic investigation; and (4) the work of art as a representation of the creative process by which it was produced.

1. THE WORK OF ART AS EXPRESSION
OF THE BIOGRAPHY OF THE ARTIST

Leonardo's depiction of the Christ Child in the presence of two maternal figures, the interest in the pyramidal configuration, and the depiction of dynamic forces which interlock figures in motion reflect the events of his own early childhood and psychological concerns over his illegitimacy. Munch's preoccupation in his work with death and sexuality, the experience of mourning, the preoccupation with illness, and fears of engulfment derive from the unhappy circumstances of his early life, the death of his mother and his sister, and the fearful fantasy of a reunion following death. In addition, some critical response, although appar-

ently dealing with works per se, may be based on an identification with the artist with whom there is a sharing of personality
attributes and conflicts. Walter Pater's ([1893] 1980) intense empathic response to Leonardo's *Mona Lisa* is based on Pater's
identification with aspects of Leonardo's own personality.

It is perhaps the case that with many works of art the bio-
graphic approach adds little to our aesthetic response although
it may add to our understanding of the factors which evoke
response. In some works, however, the artist's personality is so
much a part of the work that he expects us to derive a particular
effect from our identification with the experiences and conflicts
in his own life. Van Gogh's portraits of his bandaged head during his hospitalization after his self-mutilation (ill. 1.11) or some
of the late Rembrandt self-portraits (ill. 1.12) implicate the viewer
in the life of the artist (see chapter 5). Here it is difficult to
separate biographical reflections from aesthetic response.

2. THE WORK OF ART AS REPRESENTATION
OF UNCONSCIOUS PSYCHOLOGICAL CONTENT

Some works of art may be understood in the same way as the
manifest content of a dream; they are interpretable like manifest
elements which make their meaning clear because of the presence of associational links within the work itself. The *Bacchus*
and the *St. John the Baptist* of Leonardo, insofar as they clearly
depict androgynous males who have incorporated feminine
attributes, reveal primitive fantasies of such polymorphous psychological states. Messerschmidt's depiction of the character
heads, with their emphasis on expressive but nonemotional factors, depict the restitution phase of a psychotic process. Fragonard's *The Swing* derives its aesthetic power from its successful
delineation, through skillfully placed symbolic signifiers, of a
joyful sexual union. Posner's (1982) study is a good example of
an unmasking of formal devices in order to arrive at fundamen-

1.11 Vincent van Gogh, *Self Portrait with a Bandaged Ear* (Chicago: Private Collection).

tal meanings, perhaps conscious at the time of their depiction but subsequently undergoing repression and repudiation. It is often the case that successful psychoanalytic unmasking will reveal libidinal and aggressive undertones disguised by convenient theological or moralistic references and conventions in order to pass muster as worthy of artistic representation.

1.12 Rembrandt van Rijn, *Self Portrait* (New York: The Frick Collection).
Copyright The Frick Collection, New York.

3. AESTHETIC RESPONSE TO A WORK OF ART
AS SUBJECT FOR PSYCHOANALYTIC INVESTIGATION

The aesthetic response of a viewer—discounting idiosyncratic factors in the viewer—is an amalgam which results from the personality of the artist, the latent psychological content in a work, and the formal means available for purposes of representation. The quality of aesthetic responses varies according to the balance of content and formal factors present. Freud (1905) himself dealt with the aesthetic response in his book on jokes, where he pointed out that there is a necessary relationship between pleasure obtained through the appreciation of formal devices in art and the pleasure derived from the gratification of unconscious and repudiated desires. He gave further credit to the formal devices by pointing out that "the notion of art defies expansion as long as the quantitative proportion of unconscious material and preconscious treatment does not remain within definite limits" (E. L. Freud 1960, 449). The pleasure derived from the means of representation, i.e. the formal devices in the work such as harmony and composition, color and line, light and shape, reflect the ego's capacity to master drive and defense and tendencies toward inner disharmony and anxiety. The art object, considered from this point of view, is a result of successful problem-solving, a representation of an ego skill in ordering, expressing, and integrating.

4. THE WORK OF ART AS REPRESENTING THE
CREATIVE PROCESS BY WHICH IT WAS PRODUCED

The work of art carries a history of its own creative development. Freud's view of the *Moses* of Michelangelo suggests that the statue depicts the creative process which brought it about. Current views of art, which see art as self-referential, suggest that the artist is not only engaged in the task of creating but also depicting the pathway by which his finished product takes shape (Greenberg 1961). Artistic creativity depends on transformation of drive components in interaction with ego factors leading to an emergent synthesis.

A. Ehrenzweig (1967) has suggested that often imbedded in a work of art is a reference to the artist himself engaged in his creative task. The framing *ignudi* in Michelangelo's Sistine Ceiling are interpretable as depictions of the artist's creative urge. The increasing freedom of movement in the late *ignudi* compared to the earlier figures reflects the shift in Michelangelo's artistic personality as he worked on the ceiling over the period of several years. Thus, creativity, understood in terms of innate ability, environmental influences, and transformations of primitive psychological states and conflicts, may often be studied through the investigation of works of art which are profound expressions of the endopsychic process that gave them form.

In describing the principles of psychoanalytic iconography, I have followed a historical approach, pointing out that the rudiments of such an interpretive mode are present in Freud's works on Leonardo da Vinci and the *Moses* of Michelangelo and reach a classical expression in Kris's paper on Messerschmidt. Some contemporary scholarly studies of works of art rest on the incorporation of psychoanalysis into our Western view of the world, permitting a level of analysis of art not heretofore expressed. The interface between a psychoanalytic understanding of the artist's life and preoccupations and the unconscious content present in the work itself continues to offer an opportunity for discovering and refining the analytic tool as an instrument for understanding aesthetic response and creativity.

REFERENCES

Clark, K. 1967. *Leonardo da Vinci: An Account of His Development as an Artist.* Baltimore: Penguin.

Eggum, A. 1984. *Edvard Munch: Paintings, Sketches, and Studies.* New York: Clarkson N. Potts.

Ehrenzweig, A. 1967. *The Hidden Order of Art.* Berkeley: University of California Press.

Eissler, K. R. 1961. *Leonardo da Vinci: Psychoanalytic Notes on the Enigma.* New York: International Universities Press.

Farrell, B. 1963. On Freud's study of Leonardo. In *Leonardo da Vinci: Aspects of the Renaissance Genius,* ed. M. Philipson. New York: G. Braziller, 1966. 224–75.

Freud, E. L., ed. 1960 *Letters of Sigmund Freud.* New York: Basic Books.

Freud, S. 1899. Screen memories. *Standard Edition* 3:303–22. London: Hogarth Press.

———. 1900. *The Interpretation of Dreams. Standard Edition.* Vols. 4 and 5. London: Hogarth Press.

———. 1905. Jokes and Their Relation to the Unconscious. *Standard Edition* 7:7–122. London: Hogarth Press.

———. 1907. Delusions and dreams in Jensen's *Gradiva. Standard Edition* 9:7–95. London: Hogarth Press.

———. 1910. Leonardo da Vinci and a memory of his childhood. *Standard Edition* 11:63–137. London Hogarth Press.

———. 1914a. The *Moses* of Michelangelo. *Standard Edition.* 13:211–36. London: Hogarth Press.

———. 1914b. The history of the psychoanalytic movement. *Standard Edition* 14:7–66. London: Hogarth Press.

———. 1916–1917. *Introductory Lectures. Standard Edition.* 15–16. London: Hogarth Press.

Gombrich, E. H. 1965. The mystery of Leonardo. *N.Y. Review of Books,* 11 February, 3–5.

Greenberg, C. 1961. *Art and Culture.* Boston: Beacon Press.

Heller, R. 1978a. *Munch: The Scream.* New York: Viking Press.

———. 1978b. Edvard Munch's "Night," the aesthetics of decadence, and the content of biography. *Arts Magazine* 53:80–105.

———. 1984. *Munch: His Life and Work.* Chicago: University of Chicago Press.

Hodin, J. P. 1956. *Edvard Munch and depth psychology*. *The Norseman* 14:27–37.

Janson, H. W. 1968, The right arm of Michelangelo's "Moses." In *Festschrift für Ulrich Middledorf*, ed. A. Kosegarten and P. Tigler. Berlin: de Gruyter.

Jones, E. 1955. *The Life and Work of Sigmund Freud*. Vol. 2. New York: Basic Books.

Kris, E. [1933] 1952. *Psychoanalytic Explorations in Art*. New York: International Universities Press.

Kohut, H. 1960. Beyond the bounds of the basic rule. *J. Am. Psychoanal. Assoc.* 8:567–86.

Lichtenberg, J. D. 1978. Freud's Leonardo: psychobiography and autobiography of genius. *J. Am. Psychoanal. Assoc.* 26:863–80.

Liebert, R. S. 1983. *Michelangelo*. New Haven: Yale University Press.

Maclagan, E. 1923. Leonardo in the consulting room. *Burlington Magazine* 42:54–57.

Möller, E. 1939. Der Geburtstag des Lionardo da Vinci. *Jahrbuch der preussichen Kuntsammlungen* 60:71–85.

Panofsky, E. 1962. *Studies in Iconology*. New York: Harper and Row.

Pater, Walter [1893] 1893. *The Renaissance*. Edited by Donald L. Hill. Berkeley: University of California Press.

Posner, D. 1982. The swinging women of Watteau and Fragonard. *Art Bulletin* 54:75–88.

Schapiro, M. 1956. Leonardo and Freud: An art-historical study. *J. of the History of Ideas* 17:147–178.

Stang, R. I. 1979. *Edvard Munch: The Man and His Century*. New York: Abbeville Press.

Steinberg, L. 1983. *The Sexuality of Christ in Renaissance Art and in Modern Oblivion*. New York: Pantheon/October Books.

———. 1984. Shrinking Michelangelo. *N.Y. Rev. of Books*, 28n June 28, 41–45.

Steinberg, S., and J. Weiss. 1954. The art of Edvard Munch and its function in his mental life. *Psychoanal. Q.* 23:409–423.

Trosman, H. 1985. *Freud and the Imaginative World*. Hillsdale, N.J.: The Analytic Press.

Wohl, R. R., and H. Trosman. 1955. A retrospect of Freud's Leonardo. *Psychiatry* 18:27–39.

Wollheim, A. 1970. Freud and the understanding of art. *Brit. J. Aesthetics* 10:211–224.

2.1 Diego Velázquez, *Las Meninas* (Madrid: Museo del Prado). Alinari/ Art Resource, New York.

{ *Two* }

PSYCHOANALYSIS,

LAS MENINAS,

and the Masterpiece

Psychoanalysts who address themselves to works of art do so with a particular emphasis in mind. They are often eager to reveal some hidden components in the work which are likely to account for its psychological appeal. They are drawn to works which have an enigmatic quality, that is, to works where the attraction although intense may be mysterious and problematic. One of the early precedents in this approach is Freud's effort to solve the problem of Hamlet's procrastination, a literary crux which has perplexed readers and audiences through the centuries. The analyst has a unique contribution to make because of familiarity with the clinical situation, which provides an understanding of fundamental human themes. Recent compelling works by Milton Viederman (1987) and Ellen Handler Spitz (1994) have explored the paintings of René Magritte, and have demonstrated that many of his paintings can be understood in terms of the profound impact of his mother's suicide when he was thirteen. One can also detect in the paintings an effort to control and master feelings of loss through withdrawal and affective isolation. In some of the paintings, there is a breakthrough of primitive hostile impulses and the lost mother is visualized as an aggressive and abandoning figure—efforts to control such themes by irony and humor are recognizable to the clinical analyst.

In many applications of clinical experience to art, the analyst necessarily is indifferent to the matter of quality of the artistic work. It often seems irrelevant whether the work is any good. In passing, it may be remarked that quality occasionally does enter into our clinical assessment about case material. We sometimes speak of "rich material," "a good hour," "an incisive interpretation" as if we are making aesthetic judgments. However, generally our main concern is not with the clarity, elegance, or organizational skill with which clinical material is transmitted to us.

In addition, it is extremely difficult in applied analysis to focus solely on a work and avoid a reference to the personality of the author or artist. Analysts often feel impelled to turn from the work to the personality of the creator and to establish a linkage between the two. Here too, quality is often given short shrift. When the analyst speaks of it, he often seems to have abrogated his position as analyst and assumed a stance as sophisticated connoisseur, educated layman, or lover of art.

I would like at this point to examine—if one can hazard the expression—a "typical" masterpiece, a work of art which is universally acknowledged to be not only the supreme achievement of a great artist but also a work which has been the subject of much discussion, including psychoanalytic investigation. Perhaps in doing so we will arrive at some understanding of what we mean by a masterpiece and indeed how we might conceive of a masterpiece in a psychoanalytic sense. It may indeed be possible to assert that psychoanalysis has a contribution to make to our understanding not only to the presence of unconscious content in works of art but also to what makes a work superior to another and how this superiority can be demonstrated.

LAS MENINAS

Many people would claim that the painting *Las Meninas* by Velázquez, now in the Prado in Madrid and painted in 1656, is unquestionably a masterpiece (ill. 2.1). In fact, at the major Velázquez exhibition at the Metropolitan Museum of Art, the catalogue referred to this work as "perhaps the masterpiece of all painting" (Velázquez 1989, 52), and certainly the painting has generated a wealth of contemporary penetrating commentary and controversy (Foucault 1970; Kahr 1975; Brown 1978; Harris 1982; Snyder and Cohen 1980; Searle 1980; Steinberg 1981; Snyder 1985). It would be a hopeless task to offer a review of the entire literature, but a recent psychoanalytic article gives us an opportunity to focus our interest on the work from the perspective of depth psychology (Adams 1990). The work was painted for Philip IV of Spain while Velázquez was the court painter, and although currently entitled *The Handmaidens,* it was earlier referred to as *The Empress with Her Ladies and a Dwarf* or *The Royal Family.* We see the heir to the Spanish throne, the Infanta Margarita, who was five years old at the time. On either side of her are handmaidens, one of whom offers her a drink in a red earthenware jug, and toward the right side are a dwarf and a midget, and a dog in the foreground. Behind them is another couple, a woman and a man engaged in a conversation. In the background stands a man in the doorway, who has been identified as the queen's chamberlain. On the left side of the painting, we see the back of a huge canvas upon which the artist, Velázquez, is working. He holds a palette and a brush. We do not see directly the picture which is being painted. On the back wall is a mirror with a reflection of the king, Philip IV, and his wife, Marianna. And over the mirror are two paintings, today only dimly seen, however still identifiable. On our left is a copy of an oil sketch by Rubens entitled *The Punishment of Arachne by Minerva,* and on our right is a copy of *Apollo and Marsyas.*

To return to the figures in the foreground, the composition is structured by a number of triangles: a triangle is formed by the hands of the dwarf on the right, the back of the handmaiden on the right, and the tip of the head of the man in the doorway, which descends to the back of the handmaiden on the left. The Infanta herself is a triangle. There are reverse triangles formed by the arm and the elbow of the man in the doorway and by the left arm and brush of the painter.

An essential aspect of the painting are the gazes of the figures. The little Infanta is looking out of the painting. The handmaiden to the left looks at her, whereas the taller handmaiden also gazes out of the painting, as does the female dwarf on the right although the boy, who seems to be teasing the dog and has placed one of his feet on the back of the dog, is looking at the dog. Behind the female dwarf, the man who is dimly seen in the background seems to be gazing out of the painting, as is the man in the doorway and the painter Velázquez himself. We are soon led to surmise, as we continue to look at this work, that a narrative is in process. The looks make us aware of the fact that someone is present in front of the picture plane and that some of the figures in the painting are aware of this and some are not.

It strikes us, as we observe the exact center of the painting and see the mirror and the reflection in the mirror, that the king and queen may be in the room and the reflection in the mirror may perhaps be related to their presence. In fact, the attentive nature of the outward gazes appears to reflect the presence of royalty. Is not the taller handmaiden curtsying? Do not the female dwarf, Velázquez, and the chamberlain in the doorway look with quiet respect? Thus, gradually we are led into the construction of a story. Has Velázquez been painting a portrait of the king and queen and has the little Infanta been posing for it? Does the huge canvas, the content of which we cannot see, depict a group portrait of the family of the king and queen? Or, has Velázquez been working on a portrait of the Infanta and have the king and queen just walked into the room to observe the artist in his studio in the king's palace, painting their daughter, and do we thus see their image in the mirror?

However on further reflection and, surprisingly enough, if the geometry of the painting is worked out, the actual vanishing point to which the perspective is directed is not in the mirror on the back wall but the figure in the doorway. The orthogonal lines, when followed into the far distance, do not meet in the mirror but at the tip of the elbow of the man in the doorway (Snyder and Cohen 1980; Snyder 1985). Thus if the vanishing point is to the right of the mirror, then the mirror does not reflect figures who are standing in front of the Infanta. In fact, the image in the mirror is not a reflection of the real king and queen, who stand a little to the left of Margarita, but it is instead a reflection of the image on the canvas being painted by Velázquez. And now we have an interesting situation which seems to ring true.

In point of fact, we are in an artist's studio. The activity which we observe is the activity of painting. There are paintings all over the walls, on the right, in the back, and there is a huge canvas upon which the artist is engaged. Scholars who are inclined to interpret the work in terms of the personality of Velázquez speak of this work as a depiction of the noble art of painting. Velázquez is engaged in an activity which heightens the status of the artist and asserts the differentiation of painting as an art rather than as a craft. In fact, we know that Velázquez himself was very eager to have this distinction made, and it was very important for him to establish his eligibility for the noble Order of Santiago, the emblem of which he wears emblazoned upon his chest. This order was awarded to him in 1659, three years after the painting was started, one year before his death. It was added to the painting either by Velázquez or by someone else subsequently.

Thus, we have several ways through which we can approach the quality of this particular work. Initially, we note the complexity of its construction, the various ways in which forms are related to one another, how light is spread over the surface of the painting, how the figures relate to one another and yet at the same time relate to the composition as a whole. The painting in this sense is a combination of formal elements harmoniously related to one another and integrated into a structural totality. Simultaneously, there is a perplexity in the painting. We as viewers are made to do work, and we are confronted by the enigma of the gazes, the double question of why and to whom the gazes are directed. Even after we may feel temporarily satisfied that the respectful gazes are directed toward the king and queen, it then strikes us that the mirror image cannot be of the king and queen in actuality, that it is a reflection of the king and queen as represented on the canvas. We are confronted with a radical reorientation, the victory of divine art and the importance attached to the role of the artist. Though we as viewers are in the presence of royalty and thus privileged, it is the exemplary position attributed to the painter himself and what he is doing that is granted superior status. Without him, we would have nothing. Only he can give permanence to the fleeting events of a time long past.

What role can we ascribe to the psychoanalyst in the clarification of this work? Adams (1990) has offered a cogent interpretation using a method with which clinical psychoanalysts are familiar. She has chosen to pay particular attention to the painting of Arachne attacked by Minerva on the back wall, and we recognize that the painting is a displacement for a major oedipal theme which is not addressed directly in the foreground of the painting. The painting on the wall was done by Mazo, Velázquez's son-in-law, and is a copy of an oil sketch by Rubens. The painting depicts an event in Greek and Roman mythology which is elaborated in Book 6 of Ovid's *Metamorphoses.* Arachne, a mortal girl, had achieved acclaim for her skill as a weaver and challenged the goddess Minerva to a weaving contest, thus committing the sin of hubris. Minerva becomes incensed with the success of Arachne's tapestries, particularly since she depicts the illicit loves of Jupiter, her father. In defiance of the goddess, Arachne depicts her repudiated oedipal wishes to usurp her mother. In retribution, Minerva turns Arachne into a spider, who thus continues to spin forever.

With the help of the analysis of the myth, we may return to the depicted figures. There are two levels with which the myth and the painting on the back wall dovetail with the frontal scene in *Las Meninas.* There is a hint of oedipal rivalry in the attention received by the young Margarita and the competition with her own mother, Marianna, represented in the mirror behind her. The five-year-old Margarita was engaged at birth to the Austrian heir, and subsequent to her marriage, would return to the country from which her own mother had come. As Adams remarks, in *Las Meninas* "the queen observes her [Margarita] from front and back, perhaps keeping an eye on her as well as admiring her, and thus expresses inevitable ambivalence toward her personal oedipal rival and political successor" (Adams 1990, 607).

In addition, Velázquez himself expresses his concern about hubris. By prioritizing his *painting* of the king, rather than the king in his person, Velázquez places himself as superior to his king. Furthermore, the rival of Velázquez was Rubens. Not only was Velázquez interested in establishing the noble position of painting as an art but he was also engaged in a rivalrous competition with the great Rubens, who had preceded him to the Spanish court and was idealized as the great Northern baroque painter. Thus, by attending to the displacement represented in the painting, we increase our understanding of a major unconscious psychological theme.

There is yet another psychological theme that makes this work resonate particularly with psychoanalytic concerns of the present day. Clark (1960) approaches this theme in his analysis when he states, "our first feeling is of being there. We are standing just to the right of the king and queen" (31). There are few works of art where our sense of presence is more real. The size of the work, the scale of the figures, and the gazes of the figures give us an immediate sense of actual presence. In fact, *our* presence seems to be such a vital part of the picture we almost feel the picture cannot exist unless we are intimately involved with it. If that is so, is it possible that our presence is established through the gaze and the actions of the figures and that it is we ourselves who are represented in the reflection in the mirror? Are we the king and queen? And if indeed we are the king and queen, are we the king and queen not as we stand in front of the princess but as we are reflected from the canvas? Are we thus seeing ourselves in an ideal state, as an observed and represented ideal, in the form of fantasy? In other words, does this masterpiece reflect the importance that we now grant to the role and the position of observer, not only in any investigative process but specifically in the psychoanalytic situation? In analytic terms, we are not only the analyst who conducts the analysis, and thus observes the unconscious of the analysand, we are also the analyst as a transference figure, one upon whom the impressions from the past have been given a present form. We now think of the analytic situation as characterized by this continuous shift between observer and participant, and we see a changing interrelationship between reality, illusion, and reflection, shifts in the identification of self and object, and the vital role of the transference element in experience and perception. Just as the artist creates his illusion through the changes which he makes in what he perceives, we too mold ourselves through the creative shifts in transformations of early fantasy and personal myth. This painting speaks to us today because we have come to realize the central importance of the position of the observer and intrapsychic experience in any view of a perceptually mediated objective reality.

THE MASTERPIECE

Such reflections on Velázquez's great painting bring us to a consideration of masterpieces in general. Freud himself was not uninterested in superior quality in art. He remarked, "It can scarcely be owing to chance that three of the *masterpieces* [my italics] of the literature of all time—the *Oedipus Rex* of Sophocles, Shakespeare's *Hamlet,* and Dostoyevsky's *The Brothers Karamozov*—should all deal with the same subject, parricide. In all three, moreover, the motive for the deed, sexual rivalry for a woman, is laid bare" (1928, 188).

Freud believed that a masterpiece deals with a fundamental and essential aspect of universal human experience. That is how he thought of the oedipal complex. He made some interesting comments which account for the quality in each of the three works: he referred to the formal techniques which present the themes in terms of "softening and disguise," and "the indispensable toning down." Since it is impossible for Oedipus to acknowledge his unconscious incestuous motive, it is reality in the form of destiny or chance which motivates his encounter with his father, Laius. The parricidal wish and the murder are distanced from the fulfillment of the incestuous wish, the two cannot be manifestly related to one another. However, by introducing a further element in the myth—the destruction of the symbolic father in the form of the sphinx, who stands in his way—the consummation of the wish can then take place. The wish as an undercurrent, however, has been present all along. And after the oedipal crime is committed and revealed, it is punished as if the rational injustice of the punishment is irrelevant. In a word, the brilliance of the construction rests on the maintenance of a connecting tie between seemingly disparate and distanced elements.

A similar displacement exists in *Hamlet.* On a conscious level, the prince expresses guilt in not fulfilling his task of revenge. The guilt is displaced from guilt on a much deeper level; the parricidal impulse has been carried out by his uncle, Claudius, whom he repudiates. The prince is not overtly guilty because of his unconscious wish to commit parricide; he is guilty because of his inability to carry out his allotted task and to please his father, who has commanded him to do so. The emotional content has been turned from aggression toward obedience. The ideational content has been changed from oedipal murder to obedient revenge. The issue of quality comes up when we consider the success with which these substitutions have been made. They have to be made in some way which is recognizable and believable, yet at the same time sufficiently separated so that they are not experienced consciously as primitive, jarring, or totally unrelated. Again, the success of the work depends on the intermediate displacement.

In the past, approaches to quality in art have not taken into account this level of analysis or considered the manner in which critical psychological themes are being presented for reception. Historically, when we consider the concept of masterpiece, we find it has undergone a change of character (Cahn 1979). Initially, a masterpiece was considered an expression of the skill of an artisan. It was a chef d'oeuvre, and it entailed the production of a work which allowed an artisan to enter a guild. The notion probably arose in the mid-thirteenth century, and it was a requirement not only for makers of furniture and altarpieces, but also for cooks and barbers. In fact, often the product, that is, the masterpiece, became the property of the guild, and if appropriate, could be consumed at a nice banquet paid for by the new member. Gradually the term became extended to grace the product of *artistic* creativity, and by about 1600 the term, "masterpiece," was applied to the works of painters and sculptors as well. By the seventeenth century, the canon of ancient sculpture became the standard against which modern works were to be measured. The Medici *Venus* and the *Hercules Farnese* were the ideals of feminine beauty and the embodiment of manly strength. They were masterpieces that had endured. They had passed the test of time, and were an embodiment of genius rather than talent.

Cahn reminds us that the term could also be used in other nonartistic contexts. When on his travels Jean-Jacques Rousseau met the beautiful Zulietta in Venice, he described her in his *Confessions* as a "masterpiece of nature and love," and with her encouragement was about to make this masterpiece one of his prized possessions. However, on an intimate occasion, he noted that one of her breasts differed slightly from the other. He was so put off by this deficiency—this defect in his masterpiece—that it set off a chain of morose questions. Zulietta tried to humor him at first, but Rousseau was insistent in solving this asymmetrical formal dilemma. Finally, the beautiful courtesan covered herself over, and said, "Zanetto, lascia le donne e studia la matematica" ("Sonny, leave women alone and study mathematics") (Cahn 1979, 130).

Quality itself has been explored outside of the historical context, as well. Some have attempted to establish absolute standards of quality which go back to antiquity and have lasted for centuries, but such attempts have often been undercut by relativistic views, which emphasize how commonly judgment is affected by historical and traditional underpinnings. Idiosyncratic matters of taste have been demonstrated to subvert what had previously been thought of as an absolute and final judgment about a work. The history of culture is replete with judgments which at one time were written in stone and which a generation later became a source for embarrassment. The base of the Albert Memorial in London has carved upon it portraits of the great artists of the past and is dedicated, "To great artistic figures of the past, the great cultural leaders to whom we are all indebted, the great creators of masterworks" (Haskell 1976, plate 15). Many of the figures we would not hold in such esteem today. How, on the podium beside Velázquez, Poussin, Claude, and David, did the Baron François-Pascal Gérard manage to find a place? In J. E. Reed's *One Hundred Crowned Masterpieces of Modern Painting,* published in 1888, the works of Alma-Tadema, Cabanel, Gérome, and Meissonier are included. Appraising Rosa Bonheur's *Horse Fair* in the Metropolitan Museum, Reed asserts that "it will be considered one of the world's great masterpieces and rank with Raphael's *Transfiguration,* Rubens's *Descent from the Cross,* Leonardo's da Vinci's *Last Supper,* Michelangelo's *Last Judgment,* and (who would have guessed?) Munkaczy's *Christ before Pilate"* (Cahn 1979, 155 n.63). Who was Munkaczy?

T. S. Eliot (1944) tried to address the problem in "What Is a Classic?" and only barely could escape a historical perspective. In brief, he stated a classic could only be known by hindsight, and would be found to reflect maturity of mind, manners, or language of a particular age. Interestingly enough, he brings in the unconscious in suggesting that a balance must be present between the tradition of which one is largely unconscious and what is experienced as originality in the present. For him, Virgil was a great classical writer insofar as he expressed the maximum range of feeling of his own people.

A more recent attempt to deal with the subject of quality is J. Rosenberg's *On Quality in Art* (1967). Rosenberg's approach was to take the work of great masters and to compare them with those of minor artists or students who followed them or who worked in a similar style. He concentrated primarily on drawings, and was able to contrast the style of the master with those of the students. He found that the line in a drawing by a master would be more sensitive, the form would display more solidity or clear distinction of plane, and the composition and design would reveal more unity. There was greater artistic economy, balance, inventiveness, and originality. In making such a comparison, he attempted to set up objective criteria for quality, and concentrated primarily on formal organization as an index of artistic quality. Thus, by setting up an absolute scale, by eliminating subjectivity, and by demonstrating the presence of such objective criteria, he hoped to approach the purely aesthetic. He conceived of his method as a narrowing down necessitated by the failures of our culture. Even a generation ago, he expressed the view that the great ideals of humanity could no longer be involved in our assessment of objective art, and he advocated the concern with formal criteria of quality in order to correct the prejudices and biases which our own de-idealizing times force upon us.

Rosenberg's attempt to establish such absolute criteria did not meet with general acceptance. Ernest H. Gombrich (1968) believed it was a vain hope to search for uniform concepts of excellence and he could easily demonstrate that there were biases present in the values that Rosenberg attached to a certain work. One important bias was the belief that the artist was primarily concerned with the representation of a convincing view of perceptual reality. To a large extent, Rosenberg had neglected modern schools of expressionism, abstract expressionism, and nonrepresentational art in general. Gombrich was struck by how inadequate it often appeared to set up objective criteria, and opted for a view of excellence in terms of control and mastery. The great artist, he believed, was in supreme control of his medium. Svetlana Alpers (1972) similarly doubted whether aesthetic judgments were empirical statements, and pointed out how inseparable expressions of taste were likely to be. Indeed, she suggested that the entire issue of quality should now be of peripheral interest. Today, we should be concerned with *how* we experience a work of art rather than pontificating about the nature of what is great and what is not.

This issue brings us back to psychoanalysis, the psychological processes in the mind of the artist, and the issue of aesthetic response. Two psychoanalytic publications attempt an analysis of this problem. M. Podro (1990) in exploring some of the psychological processes in Paul Cézanne, points out the pertinence of the holding environment, what Cézanne described as holding the subject together in his mind (Winnicott 1965; Modell 1968). The artist, he said, is interested in coherence and unity, specifically a unity based on his own apperceptive qualities and not immediately related to ordinary perception. The artist provides a coherence which brings together disconnected parts. Experiences of early fusion, the balancing of the needs for harmony with the recognition of invariable disorder, and the evocation of primitive modes of perception are taken into account in the process of the artist's "making." Even the submergence of the artist's fantasies to the denseness of the medium itself is necessary in order to make the personal associations interesting.

Similarly, G. Rose (1991)—although he confines himself to abstract art—also points out that we are interested in integration of thought, feeling, and perception, and that the form this integration takes can be understood in terms of the building and resolution of tension, the rhythm which is set up between excitement and respite. He uses rhyme as a model for this integration. Variability is present yet unity exists in spite of the variability. The psychoanalyst is likely to think of early experiences of separation and individuation phases, looking to early development for an anlage for these experiences. Particularly in abstract art, we are likely to be reminded of the importance of preverbal affective readiness, "affect attunement," when we think of the origins for such things. One cannot avoid a conception of wholeness, unity, and integration as critical when we think of art. And it is through this wholeness that we experience the diphasic elements of strangeness and familiarity, change and continuity, and separation and connectedness.

Having come thus far, we can return briefly to the masterpiece, which, if we are not now so prone to give it solely an objective status, we can consider the linkage with the subjective component. Gombrich's review of Rosenberg's book on quality is titled "How Do You Know It's Any Good?" There is also a necessary question mark after the title to Kenneth Clark's book, *What Is a Masterpiece?* (1979). Such questions, we know, are likely to evoke answers which are equivocal, too general, or banal—such statements as Clark's, "The artist must be deeply involved in the understanding of his fellow men" (1979, 12), or "The highest masterpieces are illustrations of great themes" (1979, 20). It is of interest that Clark excludes pictures with an erotic theme; a masterpiece is viewed as a superb balance between sense and form, and clearly eroticism would lean too far in the direction of the sensual.

Confronted by a work of art, the viewer may have to deal with a specific response to it if he has already accepted its designation as that of a masterpiece. The aura of greatness evokes its own forceful baggage, and adds idiosyncratic dimensions to aesthetic response, which accompany idealization. The affective components—be they awe or admiration, the expectation of satisfaction or disappointment, or even hostility and envy—are likely to be derived from transference residues related to such highly invested objects which resonate with experiences from the past. Psychoanalysts can readily accept that such associative responses are ubiquitous and are always present, thus contaminating any possibility of absolute objectivity. Nor is it possible to make a clear-cut differentiation between such associative responses and those which are purely a response to the work itself. Nevertheless, such a viewpoint should not totally eliminate the view that some works are more likely to be evocative than others and that quality does not reside simply in subjectivity, but indeed has a basis in the object itself. Even if we were to throw into question the label of masterpiece and see the category as historically determined, we would not thereby eliminate from consideration the capacity of the source to produce differentiating psychological responses.

In conclusion, we might consider some accepted masterpieces from a psychoanalytic point of view. This, of course, is something that Clark himself did not do. He was content to state that a masterpiece is "by an artist of genius who has been absorbed by the spirit of the time in a way that has made his individual experiences universal" (1979, 44). Let us take some of these works and note whether our psychoanalytic perspective adds something to their understanding.

Clark (1979) includes, of course, *Las Meninas* by Velázquez. In addition to the *Las Meninas,* he lists Giotto's *Betrayal of Christ* and *Lamentation over the Dead Christ,* Botticelli's *The Birth of Venus,* Giorgione's *Sleeping Venus,* Watteau's *Embarkation for the Island of Cythera,* Raphael's *Transfiguration,* Michelangelo's *Last Judgement,* Rembrandt's *Night Watch,* Géricault's *Raft of the Medusa,* Manet's *Olympia,* and Picasso's *Guernica.* It is hard to quarrel with such a list. Many of us would think of other pictures that we would like to include: Leonardo's *Mona Lisa;* Michelangelo's *Creation of Adam* from the Sistine ceiling; Caravaggio's *Calling of St. Matthew;* pictures by Rubens, Poussin, Fragonard, and Turner; and Seurat's *Un Dimanche à la Grand Jatte.* But let us consider Clark's list.

If we start with Giotto's *Betrayal of Christ* and *Lamentation,* we are immediately struck by how appropriate it is to place the emphasis on integration of thought and feeling with various formal devices. The depiction of a betrayal through a kiss evokes for us the intimate relationship between aggression and sexuality. Psychologically, Judas incorporates the figure of Christ into his cloak through his sweeping gesture. How dramatic the scene is made for us through the various gestures and movements of the background figures and the lighted torches! In *The Lamenta-*

tion, we feel the incorporation of loss in grief as we observe the close juxtaposition of the heads of the dead Christ and the grieving mother. Botticelli's *Birth of Venus* almost seems to refute Clark's own statement that the sensual cannot be great. In fact, there is a combination of clear, sinuous line and sensuality. The emphasis on flowing line establishes the supremacy of art over sensuality. Similarly, in Giorgione's *Sleeping Venus* the sexuality may be barely contained by the form. Here, as we note how the background repeats the form of the body, we see a blending of sexuality and abstraction, where the sexuality loses nothing of its importance. In Watteau's *Embarkation for the Island of Cythera,* we experience the central role of fantasy in an idyllic world made up of dreams where an embarkation becomes a vehicle for arriving at some potentially blissful state or, as we have come to think of this work, as having left a magical place in order to return to reality, however melancholy that return may be.

Many would say that if ever there were general agreement about a masterpiece, it surely would be Raphael's *Transfiguration.* Clark, interestingly, states that in front of works like these our failures to appreciate are more a manifestation of our own deficiencies rather than any inadequacy in the work. But here, too, we can resonate on a psychological level with the experience of overcoming adversity through ascendancy and transcendence, surmounting the sense of helplessness that we as spectators feel in the presence of great events which move us deeply. Through empathic return we can respond to the universal need to deny death by a religious immersion. When we come to Géricault's *Raft of the Medusa,* we are more in the modern world, and we can appreciate the story of men who have been abandoned to their fate and, in desperate straits, cling to the hope of rescue when they feel that all is almost lost. Here, we see the domination of aggression and the related linkage with fantasies of rescue and restitution in the face of hopelessness and despair.

In the presence of Manet's *Olympia,* we enter a different phase of the modern era. Now, sexuality is not merely a dreamy erotic indulgence reflected in nature, as it was in Giorgione; it has become a personal confrontation, an area where the viewer must give an accounting and offer an explanation. Olympia, who lives in the age of Freud, asks, "Who are you? What are you looking at?" And, when we come to Picasso's *Guernica,* we again are confronted by the impact and the horror of aggression in the modern world. Again, we recognize that the artist is not merely depicting something external to himself. The figures—the actions of the bull, the horse, the broken heads, the helpless child— are the means used by the great artist to depict his own personal conflicts through a long process of working through. The personal and the external horror—the bombing of a defenseless population during the Spanish Civil War—which evoked these personal symbols, have become blended into a totality giving emotional depth to a depiction where represented reality alone would have been insufficient.

Clearly, each masterpiece is a world of its own, and has received and continues to deserve extensive commentary. Yet, it may be a unique contribution of psychoanalysis to add a new dimension to the evaluation of quality. Not only do we detect the presence of unconscious fantasy and major psychological themes in the presence of each work; we also recognize how a variety of ego mechanisms have activated formal devices which heighten the impact of the work itself. Concurrently, the works themselves then become a reservoir for the development of insight through our experience of aesthetic response.

SUMMARY

What can we abstract, then, as a summary of the relationship between psychoanalysis and an artistic masterpiece? First, an artistic masterpiece must resonate with some essential aspect of human concern. In a psychological sense, the masterpiece has the capacity to evoke and present some deeply significant emotional component which not only engages with some particularity of a historical time but also has some universal significance. In a historical sense, a masterpiece reflects major psychological preoccupations of an era. Marcel Proust's *Remembrance of Things Past* and James Joyce's *Ulysses* reflect the modern shift away from a positivist view of external reality just as Pablo Picasso's great Cubist paintings reflect a contemporary emphasis on varied and fragmented perceptual modes of observation. Insofar as masterpieces from previous historical epochs maintain their contemporary interest, however, they highlight certain basic issues which subsume historical periods.

Secondly, there is an intimate link between the ideational and emotional content of a particular work and the form with which it is presented. In a sense, the manner of presentation contains within itself the thematic content it depicts, just as in *Las Meninas* we recognize the relationship between subjectivity and observation. We note that the form of the work expresses this theme through its manner of presentation. In T. S. Eliot's poem *The Waste Land,* for example, we note the depiction of a world which has been emptied of meaning, and we are struck with how the style of presentation depicts this theme in its interrupted flow and disjunctive modes of poetic form. It is likely that following the examination of many masterpieces we find a similar blending of thematic content and formal means which then leads to an integrated aesthetic response.

Since the masterpiece is often the culmination of a lifetime of work and experience, it contains within itself an integration of concealed and deep-rooted aspects of a creator's thoughts and feelings. The process of aesthetic response repeats this process in a reverse direction, and moves from the superficial and peripheral to the essential and profound. We thus may speak of aspects of aesthetic response as a recapitulation of the control and mastery the artist has exercised in bringing together a unified and integrated work. When psychoanalysts consider a work of art in terms of psychological development, unconscious fantasy, and structural conflict, they add a dimension to the aesthetic experience and thus make a further contribution to the understanding of art.

REFERENCES

Adams, L. 1990. The myth of Athena and Arachne. *Int. J. Psychoanal.* 71:597–609.

Alpers, S. 1972. Review of J. Rosenberg, *On Quality in Art, Criteria of Excellence, Past and Present.* Princeton: Princeton University Press. *Art Bulletin* 54(1):110–13.

Brown, J. 1978. *Images and Ideas in Seventeenth-Century Spanish Painting.* Princeton: Princeton University Press.

———. 1986. *Velázquez: Painter and Courtier.* New Haven: Yale University Press.

Cahn, W. 1979. *Masterpieces.* Princeton: Princeton University Press.

Clark, K. 1960. *Looking at Pictures.* London: John Murray.

———. 1979. *What Is a Masterpiece?* Overwallop, England: Thames and Hudson.

Eliot, T. S. 1944. What is a classic? In *On Poetry and Poets.* New York: Noonday Press.

Foucault, M. 1970. *The Order of Things.* London: Tavistock Publications.

Freud, S. 1928. Dostoevsky and parricide. *Standard Edition* 21:177–94. London: Hogarth Press, 1961.

Gombrich, E. H. 1968. How do you know it's any good? *N.Y. Rev. of Books,* 1 February, 5–8.

Harris, E. 1982. *Velázquez.* Oxford: Oxford University Press.

Haskell, F. 1976. *Rediscoveries in Art.* Ithaca: Cornell University Press.

Kahr, M. M. 1975. Velázquez and *Las Meninas. Art Bulletin* 57:225–46.

Modell, A. 1968. *Object Love and Reality.* New York: International Universities Press.

Podro, M. 1990. "The landscape thinks itself in me": The comments and procedures of Cézanne. *Int. Rev. Psychoanal.* 17:401–8.

Reed, J. E. 1888. *One Hundred Crowned Masterpieces of Modern Painting.* Philadelphia: Gebbie and Co.

Rose, G. 1991. Abstract art and emotion: Expressive form and the sense of wholeness. *J. Am. Psychoanal. Assoc.* 39:131–56.

Rosenberg, J. 1967. *On Quality in Art: Criteria for Excellence, Past and Present.* Princeton: Princeton University Press.

Searle, J. 1980. *Las Meninas* and the paradoxes of pictorial representation. *Critical Inquiry* 6:477–88.

Snyder, J. 1985. *Las Meninas* and the mirror of the prince. *Critical Inquiry* 11:539–72.

Snyder, J., and T. Cohen. 1980. Reflexions on *Las Meninas:* paradox lost. *Critical Inquiry* 7:429–47.

Spitz, E. H. 1994 *Museums of the Mind: Magritte's Labyrinth and Other Essays in the Arts.* New Haven: Yale University Press.

Steinberg, L. 1981. Velázquez's *Las Meninas. October* 19:45–54.

Tolnay, C. De. 1949. Velázquez's *Las Hilanderas* and *Las Meninas. Gazette des Beaux Arts* 35:21–38.

Velázquez, D. 1989. *Exhibition Catalogue.* New York: Metropolitan Museum of Art.

Viederman, M. 1987. René Magritte: Coping with loss—reality and illusion. *J. Am. Psychoanal. Assoc.* 35:967–98.

Winnicott, D. W. 1965. *The Maturational Process and the Facilitating Environment.* New York: International Universities Press.

3.1 Giorgione, *The Tempest* (Venice: Accademia). Alinari / Art Resource, New York.

Three

THE ENIGMA OF
GIORGIONE'S *TEMPEST* AND
the Distribution of Psychic Intensity

Perhaps no work of visual art has evoked so much puzzlement or so many interpretations as Giorgione's *The Tempest* (ill. 3.1) now in the Accademia, Venice. The work belongs to the Venetian Renaissance, and was painted between 1506 and 1509, the most likely year being 1508, about two years before the death of Giorgione. The painting depicts three figures in a landscape. A seminude woman with a child she is breast-feeding sits on a knoll on the right. Toward the left stands a man holding a staff, dressed as a courtier, looking in her direction but not directly at her. In the background, we see a stormy sky with a bolt of lightening. The landscape also contains an architectural setting with buildings in the background. In the middle distance, a bridge crosses the scene over a body of water, and there is a small body of water in the foreground as well. It is not clear whether the two are connected. In the right foreground there is a snake, half-hidden by a rock.

Controversy has surrounded this picture and Giorgione almost from the very beginning. Giorgio Vasari, writing in the middle of the sixteenth century, a few decades after the death of Giorgione, did not comment directly about *The Tempest*. He did refer, however, to frescoes Giorgione had done for the Fondaco dei Tedeschi (the German warehouse near the Rialto Bridge in Venice). Giorgione had painted some figures on the warehouse facing the Grand Canal, and Vasari stated, "I for my part have never understood his figures nor have I found for all the inquiries that I have made anyone who understands them" (Vasari 1568, 798). More recently, and referring directly to *The Tempest*, Clark (1976) states, "No one knows what it represents" (115). The uncertainty about the subject matter has not interfered with fascination with this particular painting. In fact, the puzzle has served to whet the appetite and has produced a plethora of interpretations, particularly during the last century and a half. In this chapter, I shall first deal with the various types of interpretation. I shall then examine certain qualities about the nature of the work itself which encourage and maintain disparate readings, and suggest psychoanalytic explanations for its evocative nature.

Attempts to deal with the picture have centered around the topic of whether or not the painting has narrative content. Content in this sense does not refer simply to a description of the fact that the figures exist within a landscape. Those who claim a subject matter maintain that the figures form part of an allegory or a narrative, depicting a historical event or a theme. Perhaps the theme has a meaning which is hidden, either because we do not understand some literary reference which was clear at the time of conception or there was a deliberate attempt on the part of the artist to depict a subject discernable only to a select few. Another possibility is that there is an unconscious intent in the evident concealment. The artist may have depicted a scene which is decipherable in terms of modern psychological knowledge but was not conscious to the artist himself or his audience. Thus, the painting is similar to other enigmatic works of art, such as the problem plays of Shakespeare, the *Mona Lisa*, or Michelangelo's *Moses* (Freud 1910, 1914). With regard to a visual work of art, insofar as literary sources in the form of contemporary documents such as commissions or letters are absent, the interpretation of enigmatic content is not an easy task.

It is also possible to consider an interpretation of *The Tempest* which considers the painting as having no theme in its manifest content or, in any case, to attach less significance to the importance of the subject than to the manner in which it is presented. In this sense it would resemble, for example, an impressionist landscape by Monet, which is not distinguishable in terms of its narrative content or the complexity of ideational thought associated with the landscape. Here, too, a psychoanalytic point of view may discern aspects of the work which play a role in producing a variety of responses similar to the effect brought about by abstraction. However, when we consider the literature on *The Tempest*, we find that many of the interpretations of the painting concern themselves primarily with its allegorical, narrative, or historical content and consider the subject matter as primary.[1]

The first recorded comment about the painting was made in 1530 by Marcantonio Michiel, a near contemporary of Giorgione who saw the painting in the house of the well known family in Venice, the Vendramin. Michiel described the painting as "a landscape with a tempest, gypsy woman and a soldier" (Richter 1937, 5). The painting was not referred to again in the literature until 1855, when Jacob Burckhardt, the great Swiss historian, described it as a depiction of *Giorgione's Family*. Since that time, for the past century and a half, there has been a constant flood of interpretations (Settis 1990).[2]

A favored interpretation has been to read the scene in terms of ancient classical mythology. One of the earliest of the mythological interpretations was that attempted by Wickhoff in 1895, who

1. A publication by S. Settis (1990) has presented a comprehensive and critical account of the many interpretations to which the painting has been subjected. Settis himself offers an interpretation, which I shall discuss subsequently. The reader who wishes to familiarize himself with the many interpretations is advised to turn to Settis's book. I shall summarize the general form of the interpretations, and deal with some of the specific ones where appropriate.

2. Settis has tabulated many of these interpretations on pages 78–79 of his publication.

interpreted the painting as a scene from the *Thebais* of the Latin poet Statius. Wickhoff saw the scene as one in which the Greek hero Adrastus, in search of water, comes upon Queen Hypsipyle suckling the child Opheltes. In the myth, the serpent bites Opheltes, who then dies. Although Wickhoff accounts for the presence of the man, woman, child, and the serpent, the myth says nothing about the presence of a storm.[3] On the grounds that a proper interpretation should account for every significant part of the painting, Wickhoff's view is rejected by many others.

Others, particularly Eisler (1946), have suggested that the painting is a portrayal of the exposure of Paris on Mount Ida. Klauner (1955) and Battisti (1960) also cite classical mythology and see the lightning as the thunderbolt of Zeus. Klauner regards the picture as a representation of the birth of Dionysus. Zeus visits Semele, who becomes pregnant, and she is destroyed by the power of his thunderbolt; the child of this union is then raised by Semele's sister Ino, who becomes the wet nurse to the god. The man in the picture represents Hermes, who serves as a messenger and protector of the god.[4] Battisti also saw the theme as a story depicting Zeus's love, but for Io rather than Semele. Here again, the thunderbolt stands for the presence of Zeus. Such mythological interpretations—and there are many more—give an inkling of the attempt at setting up a mythological and narrative story that would account for the presence of the figures in the scene. Giorgione is assumed to have been familiar with

3. Settis makes the important point that in order to substantiate a narrative, it would be necessary to account for every single element in the painting, i.e., the presence of the man, the woman and the child, the serpent, and the storm. Any interpretation which leaves out any of these critical elements thus would be noncomprehensive.

4. X rays have revealed that in place of the man on the left side of the picture there was a female figure, who was seated on the bank of the river, and that Giorgione painted over this figure to create the standing male whom we now see. It has been assumed that, since Hermes took Dionysus to nymphs who dwelt at Nysa, the earlier female figure was a representation of one of the nymphs at Nysa.

classical antiquity or his patrons may have suggested the myth to him and he followed their instruction. Judging from the visual evidence and in the absence of actual historical documents to support a commission, it would be very difficult to establish with any certainty that any particular myth is being depicted.

Another important contribution was Edgar Wind's *Giorgione's "Tempest" with Comments on Giorgione's Poetic Allegories* (1969). Wind had been interested in pointing out the presence of pagan mysteries in Renaissance painting. However, when he came to write about *The Tempest,* he abjured a narrative interpretation in favor of an allegorical one. He believed that there was an air of unreality and unrelatedness about the figures in *The Tempest* which is incompatible with narrative; since there is so little inter-action, there is little basis for the telling of the story. He dis-missed the importance of a concealed nude woman which has been revealed by X ray to have been painted under the man on the left side of the canvas as an indicator of a prior narrative. Wind suggested that Giorgione may simply have reused the canvas, much as Gainsborough painted the *Blue Boy* over the partially painted portrait of a middle-aged man, the image of whom has also been detected by X ray.

Wind proposed that several elements of the painting have an allegorical relationship to a particular Renaissance theme. The broken column stands for Fortitude, and the presence of the columns next to the standing man—who may be interpreted as a soldier—heightens the emphasis on strength and manly virtue. The tempest represents Fortune. The nude woman who suckles the child stands for Charity. What is the Renaissance theme? Fortezza and Carita can withstand the uncertainty of Fortuna. Charity and strength of will can overcome adversity. Thus, *The Tempest* is a pastoral allegory; Giorgione has given the landscape significant stature commensurate with its allegorical weight.

Although supported by some scholars, Wind's interpretation, which depends on a linear symbolization, is criticized by others.

Settis (1990) denies that the unbroken columns represent Fortitude or solidity, and suggests instead that they represent death, particularly the death of paganism. Waterhouse (1974), who finds an allegorical approach alien, writes that one of the few things that he feels convinced about concerning Giorgione is that "his mind was very unlike that of Professor Wind" (4). In other words, Giorgione was too much of a lyrical poet to think in terms of such rigid analogies.

In 1972, De Grummond suggested that the male figure is St. Theodore, the patron saint of Venice before St. Mark was given this role. The legend of St. Theodore tells the story of a saint whom Christ told to fight a dragon outside a city in Asia Minor. St. Theodore reached the city as the son of a poor Christian widow was about to be sacrificed. The saint kills the dragon. De Grummond claims that the image of the dragon appears on a distant tower in the background. Others claim that the figure that one sees with some difficulty refers to the "lion of St. Mark." The lightning in this interpretation of the painting is bypassed, and thus one of the essential aspects of the painting cannot be accounted for.

Other interpretations of a similar mythological and religious nature have been proposed. Recently there has been an interest in seeing *The Tempest* in terms of its historical and political context. Howard (1985) suggests that the painting can be related to an impending contemporary military struggle. The League of Cambrai had been formed to punish Venice for aggressive policies on the mainland, and in 1508 Venice felt threatened by the loss of mainland territory and the possibility of invasion. Kaplan (1986), who dates *The Tempest* to 1509, suggests that the painting commemorates the Venetian conquest and defense of Padua. He sees the impending storm as a sign of war and unpredictable fortune, and suggests that Giorgione's probably patron, Gabriele Vendramin, had a great interest in commemorating the war because of the martial tie of his brothers and uncle, both of whom fought in it.

Settis, after a thorough critique of the various prior interpretations up to 1978, offers one of his own. He points out that Giorgione tended to turn religious themes into secular ones and gave a contemporary philosophical dimension to sacred stories. Science and philosophy, as well as theology, could offer a pathway through which a man of his time could find God. *The Tempest,* suggests Settis, depicts God's warning to Adam and Eve following the expulsion from the Garden of Eden. The man and woman in the foreground are Adam and Eve. The thunderbolt represents the presence of God, broken columns foretell the individual death of man and woman following the expulsion. "In the glare of lightning God decrees a destiny of toil and pain to men and women. . . . henceforth death will cut short the lives of all men" (Settis 1990, 112); "The man, Adam, pauses in his work to reflect on the fate of all mankind" (114); "The baby is Cain. Adam and Eve are brooding over the consequences of their trespass" (118); "An old theme has been brought into the present through Adam's modern dress" (125).

In addition, Settis proposes that Giorgione had an interest in purposefully concealing the meaning of the painting so that only a select few would understand its theme. The select few, an aristocratic intellectual Venetian set, who could tolerate the secularization of religious themes, wished to dissociate themselves from the uneducated, and symbolism became a means for effecting this concealment. Thus, God is painted not as represented in human form as in the Sistine Chapel ceiling, but is signified by a thunderbolt. The Garden of Eden is represented by the city buildings in the background. By giving the theme of the expulsion of Adam and Eve an updated form, Giorgione thus was able to use the theme as an elegiac and melancholic connection to a lost paradise and to the theme of a humanity divorced from its primordial origins.

The contribution of Settis, although developed with care, is subject to the same criticism as that attached to other iconographic interpretations. There are no documents or literary references about the painting which clearly establish a link between the subject matter and the theme of expulsion from paradise. There is a vast difference between *The Tempest* and the expulsion theme as represented in Michelangelo's Sistine Chapel, where there is no question about the subject. In an earlier version of the expulsion in the familiar frescoes for the Brancacci Chapel in Santa Maria del Carmine, Florence, we see the angel with the fiery sword over the naked Adam and Eve. In Giorgione, there is no angel, no sword, and no casting forth.

At this point, I would like to consider views of the painting which are less concerned with subject matter and storytelling and more with mood, emotion, and the specific manner in which Giorgione expressed his aesthetic.

It has been aptly stated that with Giorgione we see the beginning of the so-called modern manner, that is, that type of painting in which there is a decline in the importance of the subject in favor of formalist concerns, painting which we associate today with abstraction. To a large extent, Giorgione gives up the link with the pictorial and literary tradition of the past, and his work becomes the product of his own wishes and his imagination. He "uses subjects as means to express his ways of feeling and seeing and in *The Tempest* we see for the first time a landscape with figures rather than figures in a landscape" (Venturi 1962, 335). The scene, in a word, contributes to the overall effect, and there is a loss of distinction between foreground and background.

Consideration of *The Tempest* from a psychoanalytic point of view must take into serious consideration the contribution of Adrian Stokes (1902–1972). Stokes was an English critic and painter who wrote extensively on art. He "has a secure reputation as one of the most remarkable English writers on art of our century, and this reputation is underscored by the fact that he was perhaps the first critical writer of note ... wholeheartedly and unreservedly to accept the relevance of psychoanalytic method to his work" (Bann 1988, 134). The psychoanalytic point of view became an influence when, in 1930, following a period of intense depression in his late twenties, Stokes entered psychoanalysis with Melanie Klein. Subsequently, his work became progressively influenced by Kleinian psychoanalytic thinking, and his later writings reflect this point of view.

Stokes was a great lover of Italy, and traveled there frequently in the 1930s during interruptions of his analysis. At the time that he wrote of *The Tempest*, in 1945, he had not seen his beloved Venice for at least six years, and thus he wrote of the picture toward the end of the war and largely from memory without recent observation.

For Stokes, *The Tempest* is "one of the most extraordinary of man's creations" (Stokes 1978 2:127). It reveals, he claimed, a feeling of suspended action evoked by a leveling interest between the figures and the landscape. Although there is a sense of a bond between the man and the woman, it is no greater than the link with the landscape. The man looks past the woman, and the woman looks out at the spectator, and they are divided by a stream linked to each other and the landscape itself in equal measure. Stokes was primarily impressed with the calmness and the sense of ease of the painting. He assumed that the woman who suckles the infant ("an action of primal importance," 129) had previously bathed in the stream and is not yet altogether dry. The act of suckling induces a sense of calm and self-sufficiency upon the spectator.

He pointed out that the most important quality of the painting is the fact that the flash of light, which illuminates the evening scene, adds an intensity to the color of each particular element in the painting. The strong local color, given a heightened intensity by the effect of light, produces a sense of permanence to a scene characterized by the impermanence of the lightning. Through the use of light and color, the external world has become a repository for the emotions of the artist.

Stokes finds some support for his emphasis on calmness and

tranquility in Vasari's comments about Giorgione and his personality. He was considered to be a charming companion, a fine singer who enjoyed playing upon the lute, of a lyrical disposition. It is this inner personality which is projected into the work. The focus on the inner world, which is expressed in outward form, can be considered as the result of the Kleinian experience and the emphasis that the Kleinian school has given to the visual arts. In this regard, the high value Stokes associates with the mother-child unit adds content to this formal conception. However, others, particularly those interpreters who have read the work in terms of the effect of the threat to Venice in the Cambian wars, have stressed a quality of vulnerability in the figures, suggesting that the scene is not one of the ease which Stokes described but carries a sense of threat, isolation, and vulnerability (Howard 1985). In any case, Stokes could find in the contemplation of *The Tempest* a confirmation of his view that art was a projection of an inner fantasy world. He wrote, "the external world is the sounding board of the emotions. That is self-evident: nevertheless, in contemplating the eternal poetry of Giorgione's *Tempesta*, it has seemed a discovery" (Bann 1988, 143).

It is eminently clear that this small Giorgione painting has continued to interest many and to evoke a wide variety of interpretations and approaches. On a direct visual level, we are struck by the presence of a man and a woman and a child in a stormy landscape. The picture depicts a familial grouping, and the early designation of this painting as Giorgione's family may be an indication that prior to iconographic analysis there was already an appreciation of a nuclear content. If we think, then, of a family in a generic sense, then Settis's view that this is the first family, the primordial family, may indeed have some pertinence since, as he also states, we identify ourselves with that first family. Certainly the presence of a stormy landscape represents the possibility of vulnerability and threat. The man with his staff, whether he is a soldier or a shepherd (Hale 1988), is a representation of protection in the face of threat, and the woman and the suckling child are clearly the object of protection and the need for support.

From the point of view of contemporary aesthetic response, it is questionable whether a more specific mythological narrative would heighten the impact of the work. We can react, in fact, to the generic family, with whom we are identified, with a greater degree of responsiveness if the figures are not identifiable as representations of specific mythological figures. The nonidentifiability of the figures creates opportunities for projection and internalization, much as the neutral analyst in the analytic situation becomes a target for the attachment of transferences.

Of equal importance to the nondefinability of the figures is the quality of evenhandedness with which color and light are distributed. Each area of the surface retains a local color giving the scene a lack of recession with depth. In fact, the lightning heightens the brightness of the colors in the background so that the usual tendency to see objects in the background as darker is reversed. The tree in the landscape in the foreground is darker than others in the back. If each element in the painting is given equal weight and no one specific element has more emphasis attached to it than another, opportunities for projection become even greater. We react to the work in a manner similar to our response to an abstract painting. Figures and landscape become qualities of equivalent intensity, allowing passage of interest from one area to another.

In this regard, an aspect of the painting which is often overlooked is the bridge in the middle distance. The bridge spans the painting mainly horizontally and slightly vertically, connecting the area behind the man to the area behind the woman. Thus the bridge not only connects the human figures, it also acts as a unifying link between the various aspects of the picture, each of which carries its own separate valence: the lightning at the top and the snake at the bottom, the man on one side, the woman on the other, the trees in either direction, the buildings in the background, and the stream in the foreground. In a similar fashion, there is a pairing of the man and his staff, the two truncated columns next to one another, and the woman and the child.

The empowering of an external object with subjective value certainly is familiar to the clinical psychoanalyst, and is a characteristic of the psychoanalytic process. The analyst, by consciously not taking sides, permits ease of representability and opportunities for projection and investment of intrapsychic fantasy in both analyst and analysand. The less endowed the analytic situation is with qualities inherent in reality, the more evocative the situation is for a functional and controlled projection of an internal fantasy world. Transference itself is a phenomenon which makes use of the presence of a more or less neutral field, permitting attachments of internal content to perceptual intrusions by external reality (Franklin 1990).

The multiple interpretations we see in a painting such as *The Tempest* are an indication of the phenomenon of the fundamental quality of representability present in the painting itself. At the same time, however, the range and variety of interpretations are an indication that the painting is not a tabula rasa, much as the analyst has come to accept this view with regard to the clinical situation.

We might well ask, keeping in mind the analytic situation, what aspects of a painting such as *The Tempest* we are more likely to respond to even though the emphasis is on equivalence. Clearly, the human figures are likely to evoke some identificatory responses simply on the basis of being human. In this regard, one might well agree that for transference and countertransference to occur in the analytic situation the human attributes are essential. In the sense that relational aspects are also of importance, these draw attention as well. One could plot a sequence of gazes of *The Tempest* by following a pathway of eye contacts—from the man toward the woman, from the woman toward the spectator of the scene, from the spectator toward the lightning, from the lightning to the bridge, water and snake and back to the figures—all of which are kept in the form of suspended tension through distribution of color and light in balance. In repeating such a process, a contemporary beholder may soon experience the painting as a repository for the attachment of components of an internal world. One such component is the attraction exercised upon the distribution of attention cathexis. Here, we are dealing with an interplay between external content which exerts a pull on perceptual attention and the push from internal sources which alerts the observer to particular cues. It appears highly likely that the painting served this function for Adrian Stokes when, subsequent to his analysis, he understood the importance of the depicted visual image as a representational arena for psychic content.

James Joyce described an epiphany as the "sudden revelation of the whatness of a thing" (Ellmann 1959, 87). Joyce was much taken by the notion that common objects could be discovered to have a quality of imminence associated with them and that it was the job of the artist to describe such revelations, which he observed in speech, gesture, or image, giving an affective charge to mundane experience. The quality of sensory reality associated with such experiences has similarities to the dream experience. Components in *The Tempest* derive intensity as a result of the mechanisms of the dream work such as condensation and displacement, just as elements in the manifest image in the dream of necessity are encoded similarly with sensorial attributes. Such empowerment of intensity is present in *The Tempest*. Is the image of the man that of a soldier? Michiel thought so. Hale (1988) found ample evidence for the fact that he cannot be a soldier; he is much more likely to be a shepherd. Is he at ease? Stokes thought so. Does he communicate a sense of being threatened, filled with fear and foreboding? Howard (1985) thought so.

Clearly, primary process mechanisms are at play, and logically contradictory interpretations can be present. The scope of interpretation is secondary to the presence of enigmatic content, yielding to a widened capacity for the evocation of fantasy. Indeed, in the final analysis what we are witnessing is the capacity of a great artist to present to us the process of fantasy formation itself, the conditions under which it can be produced, that it can be transmitted, and that it lends itself to the continuing process of renewal and recreation in the mind of the viewer.

SUMMARY

Giorgione's painting *The Tempest* has stirred a wealth of diverse interpretations. A psychoanalytic perspective gives a clue to the enigmatic quality of the work. The nature of the equivocal tie between the figures heightens the tie to the landscape. The landscape, particularly the bridge, serves as a visual and relational link and attains a significance equivalent to the human figures. The establishment of a neutral equivalence encourages the projection of an internal fantasy world in balance.The painting presents an elemental familial relationship under threat, the basis upon which production of fantasy occurs.

REFERENCES

Bann, S. 1988. Adrian Stokes: English aesthetic criticism under the impact of psychoanalysis. In *Freud in Exile: Psychoanalysis and Its Vicissitudes*, ed. Edward Timms and Naomi Segal. New Haven: Yale University Press.

Battisti, E. 1960. *Rinascimento e Barocco*. Turin: G. Einaudi.

Burckhardt, J. 1855. *Der Cicerone: Eine Anleitung zum Genuss der Kunstwerke Italiens*. Stuttgart: Kröner.

Clark, K. 1976. *Landscape into Art*. New York: Harper and Row.

De Grummond, N. T. 1972. Giorgione's "Tempest": The Legend of St. Theodore. *L'arte* 18–19/20:5–53.

Eisler, R. 1946. Letter. *Times Literary Supplement* XLV:66.

Eliot, T. S. 1944. What is a classic? In *Poetry and Poets*. New York: Noonday Press.

Ellmann, R. 1959. *James Joyce*. London: Oxford University Press.

Franklin, G. 1990. The multiple meanings of neutrality. *J. Am. Psychoanal. Assoc.* 38:195–220.

Freud, S. 1910. Leonardo da Vinci and a memory of his childhood. *Standard Edition* 11:63–137. London: Hogarth Press.

———. 1914. The *Moses* of Michelangelo. *Standard Edition* 13:211–36. London: Hogarth Press.

Hale, J. 1988. Michiel and the Tempesta: The soldier in a landscape as a motif in Venetian painting. In *Florence and Italy: Renaissance Studies in Honour of Nicolai Rubinstein*, ed. Peter Denley and Caroline Elam. London: Westfield College, University of London, Committee for Medieval Studies.

Howard, D. 1985. Giorgione's *Tempesta* and Titian's *Assunta* in the context of the Cambrai wars. *Art History* 8:271–89.

Kaplan, P. H. D. 1986. The storm of war: The Paduan key to Giorgione's Tempesta. *Art History* 9:405–27.

Klauner, F. 1955. *Jahrbuch der kunsthistorischen sammlungen in Wien* LI:165, n. 80.

Richter, G. M. 1937. *Giorgi da Castelfranco.* Chicago: University of Chicago Press.

Settis, S. 1990. *Giorgione's Tempest: Interpreting the Hidden Subject.* Chicago: University of Chicago Press.

Stokes, A. 1978. *The Critical Writings of Adrian Stokes.* 3 vols. London: Thames and Hudson.

Vasari, G. 1568. *Lives of Eminent Painters, Sculptors and Architects.* Translated by Gaston du C. de Vere. New York: H. N. Abrams, 1912–1914.

Venturi, L. 1962. Giorgione. *Encyclopedia of World Art* 6:327–39.

Waterhouse, E. 1974. *Giorgione.* Glasgow: University of Glasgow Press.

Wickhoff, F. 1895. Giorgiones Bilder zu römischen Heldengedichten. *Jahrbuch der königlichen preussischen Kunstsammlungen* XVI:334–43.

Wind, E. 1967. *Pagan Mysteries in the Renaissance.* 2nd ed. New York: W. W. Norton.

———. 1969. *Giorgione's "Tempest" with Comments on Giorgione's Poetic Allegories.* Oxford: Oxford University Press.

4.1 Georges Seurat, *Un Dimanche à la Grande Jatte* (Chicago: The Art Institute of Chicago). Courtesy of The Art Institute of Chicago.

{ Four }

SEPARATION AND
COHESION IN SEURAT'S
Un Dimanche à la Grande Jatte

When the distinguished art historian, John Pope-Hennessy, visited the Art Institute of Chicago in the 1960s, he admired the progressive educational program. He observed a class in action, and watched a group of children being "persuaded to enter that most impenetrable of great paintings, Seurat's *Grande Jatte*." The instructor asked what day of the week was being represented, and they correctly guessed Sunday. They were asked which forms were straight and which were curved, and they correctly pointed out that the women were curved and the men and the trees were straight. And then they were asked, "How far can you see?" The children were silent, "and then one little girl got up and, in a voice trembling with emotion, replied: 'Real far.'" (Pope-Hennessy 1991, 181)

In this chapter, I propose to increase our depth of vision into *La Grande Jatte* through the use of a psychoanalytic perspective. I describe the painting in some detail, and offer an analysis of the work from the point of view of art historians who have interpreted it from formal and iconographic perspectives. I focus on an interpretation which highlights the psychological dimension, and offer some biographical material dealing with the life and personality of Seurat, paying particular attention to how his

[89]

personality was reflected in a critical interaction with his friend, the post-impressionist critic, Félix Fénéon. Lastly, I focus on the means of representation by which Seurat was able to achieve his aesthetic effect.

Georges Seurat's painting *Un Dimanche à la Grande Jatte* (ill. 4.1), which was started in 1884 and completed in 1886, has increased in importance as the years have gone by. It is now recognized not only as a great masterpiece but as a transitional work in a number of senses. It points to a critical shift in the impressionist movement and an increasing interest in structure and organization in works of art. It marks a shift in the preoccupation with studying nature and one's perceptions of nature on-site and a return to traditional and classical modes of painting nature. Yet, paradoxically, it moves away from certain classical forms and adopts a style which in many ways can be considered modernist in that it is based on "scientific" studies of the effects of color and light on the retina and of how pigments can be applied to a canvas in order to assure a maximum of optical effect. In addition, the thematic content speaks to our time. Some critics have judged the work a critique of society, a pessimistic view of isolated people engaged in a meaningless activity characterized by anomie and alienation, bored with life and concerned largely with appearances rather than psychological realities. Others have seen the painting as a beautiful evocation of relaxation and ease, a nostalgic return to a happy time of childhood.

Although Pope-Hennessy described the painting as "impenetrable," his view detracts very little from the fact that indeed much is presented to us, both in terms of content and form. A description of what we see may be a psychoanalytic entrée just as the content of an analytic session is an entrée into the deeper meaning of what we hear.

It is a Sunday afternoon, and we are in an island recreational park which was set aside for the leisure of the Parisian middle class. No one is working. Many are dressed in attractive clothes. From our knowledge of the site, we know that the sun is about to sink on our left. We are looking north, and it is about four o'clock in the afternoon. In the immediate foreground a couple has entered from the right; the woman and man are both rigid and upright. She carries a parasol and supports a large bustle and a monkey on a leash that she holds in her left hand. The man is smoking a cigar, and carries a cane under his right arm. We see the puffs of smoke from his cigar wafting into the middle distance. When we look carefully, we note the man wears a monocle. The couple is moving toward the left at a leisurely pace through the shaded area. Toward the left of the painting in the foreground there is a group of three people: a man in the foreground is dressed as a boatman, smoking a pipe; behind him there is a small man holding a cane, dressed in a top hat like a dandy; behind him sits a woman who is sewing, and she has a book, a parasol, and a fan beside her. And behind her is a dark mongrel pursued by a dainty pug with a ribbon around his neck. Behind these foreground figures there are about forty other figures, grouped in various ways.

On the left is a woman fishing. She stands at the water's edge, and she too has a big bustle, fashionable at the time. Beside her, another woman sits on the ground. Nearby there is a crooked tree with a nurse who sits in front of it and an old woman who shades herself with a parasol as she sits in the sun. In the center of the painting, and seemingly advancing toward us, there is a child—probably a girl—in a light dress and beside her a woman, likely her mother, who also shades herself with an parasol. On their right there are two women, one with another parasol and one who sits behind her holding a bouquet of flowers, and beside her there is her parasol and a hat. Toward the far right of the painting and behind the two large figures in the right foreground, there is a perambulator with three figures in front of it, a child and two women. A young girl is running toward the perambulator and the figures, and is the only one of all of the human figures in the painting who shows any active movement.

As we move into the background, we see a number of figures in a variety of positions. On the left, behind the old woman and the nurse, stands a man who is blowing a trumpet. Two women are on the grass behind him, one sits and one lies in a recumbent position. There are two cadets behind them in stiff postures. Do they jump to attention when they hear the sound of the man's trumpet? To the right are two more solitary figures: a woman with a white parasol, a man who sits with his back against a large tree. Toward the right of the tree there are a man and a woman, and the man carries a baby to whom the woman is attending. As we move back and farther to the right, a man and a woman with a white parasol walk away from us, and in the far distance there is a solitary figure with a parasol behind them. Our eye then moves to the left again. We see solitary sticklike figures in front of the trees in the background and then a number of figures in the river along with sailboats, ferryboats, a few figures facing outward toward the river, and a number of boats. One is a steamboat belching smoke. There is a crew of four with a figure shaded by a white parasol who sits in front of the rowers, another man who fishes in the water, and another sailboat toward the left-hand margin, another ferryboat with steam belching from the funnel, and a solitary figure sitting in the boat. Toward the back of the scene there is a white wall with a number of rectangular structures perched behind it. Some of these are reflected in the water, as are the vessels.

The painting communicates an atmosphere of immobility, tranquility, and fixity. The figures are carefully placed, and apparently much thought has been accorded to their placement. Of the forty or so figures in the painting, most of them are women, and this is in marked contrast to Seurat's other large painting of this time, *Une Baignade*—a painting of the opposite bank of the river—where all the figures are men. In contrast to *Une Baignade*, where the figures are looking off to the right, many of the figures in *La Grande Jatte* are looking off to the left. In contrast to the figures in *Une Baignade*, here the figures seem to vary in dress although most are in their "Sunday best."

We might do well to examine the structure of the painting and the placing of the shapes. First, there is a flatness to the shapes. There is no attempt to model the figures or to present them as volumetric. The figures in the immediate foreground, the three on the left and the two on the right, look as if they are flats on a stage set. Thus, there is a quality of impenetrability about the painting—the quality Pope-Hennessy referred to—as if we are brought up short against the initial figures and they bar our passage until we manage to get past them. We are helped a bit by the little pug dog in the foreground who moves in depth as he rushes toward the mutt on the left. Another factor in inducing the movement of our eye is created by the recessing diagonals that are set up from the right to the left and from the left to the right. One diagonal consists of the two standing figures on the right, followed by the two seated women, followed by the child and the mother, followed by the two women lying on the ground, followed by the two cadets, a series of five couples— the man and woman, the two women, the woman and child, the two women, and the two men. Both groups of seated figures consist of two women. The other diagonal extends from the left to the right: the group consisting of the boatman, the dandy, and the sewing woman is in line with the women in the center who are linked to the three figures sitting in front of the perambulator. Here, too, our eye moves along a diagonal but not as deeply into the background as the diagonal that stretches from right to left. Quite clearly, a great deal of attention has been placed to the structural placement of the figures. No one in the painting looks directly out at the viewer except the child in white, who is in dead center.

We note also how the painting is framed in two ways: first by a swatch of green on the upper edge of the painting, made up of the foliage on the trees, and the shade of the green grass in the lower foreground. The two darker shades of green separate out an area consisting of similar smaller horizontal green areas, which represent the shadows of the figures in the middle ground, and the shadows look as if they are pedestals upon which the figures are standing. The light and dark colored areas bring to mind how important the issues of color and light were for the artist and how striking they are in producing their visual effect. We now know that the somewhat brownish patches in the center, which were added later, represent a deterioration in the bitumen paint Seurat applied. This was originally a bright orange but soon lost its brilliance because of exposure to atmospheric changes.

Color in general was a source of great technical interest for Seurat. He took pride in having devised a formal approach to painting, which he called chromo-luminism, also referred to as divisionism or pointillism, and was based on color theories of the time. Small areas of primary colors, such as yellow and blue, placed near each other at a proper distance were thought to fuse in the retina to create green. Also, by juxtaposing complementary colors he believed he could heighten the visual effect through their combined impact. A red juxtaposed to a green or to a violet would increase the value of each. It was believed some of the colors carried an emotional impact and the usual distinction between warm and cool colors would create a subjective resonance through judicious placement. In addition, pigments were applied with small brush strokes or dots in a methodical and careful manner, which also heightened luminosity and hence the visual impact. The artist took great pride in these technical advances and saw them as a progression from the spontaneous and unstructured "broken" brushwork of the impressionists. Seurat emphasized that his paintings depended on "a method," and in this way he saw himself as drawing nearer to the thought of contemporary scientists, who had also perfected a scientific method which aided them in their laboratory experiments.

La Grande Jatte has been studied extensively not only in terms of its technical innovations but also in terms of its content. How are we to interpret the actions of the various figures and the scene they inhabit? The facial expressions are impassive, most of the figures are looking out of the picture, their groupings are ambiguous, and the relationships among the people seem distant. In fact, the method of painting, with dabs and flecks which cover large areas of the canvas with a similar quality, abnegates the relative value of the humans depicted (House 1980). The mechanical reiteration of short brush stroke and the dot is anti-expressive. The figures appear frozen and isolated. Signs of movement are minimal (Nochlin 1989). Perhaps the most cogent comment about the content of the painting is by Herbert et al. (1991): "A dialogue of cohesion and separation constitutes the convincing interpretation of *La Grande Jatte*" (177). Herbert argues that the general emphasis on the isolation and alienation of the characters in the painting is corrected by the artist's interest in the harmonious integration of the form. In fact, *La Grande Jatte* embraces both isolation and integration. People are subordinated to the community of forms he constructs, but the cohesiveness does not become a total abstraction. The separate units continue to be visible, each image has a determined place; even though the figures may not be relating to one another, particularly in the foreground, no one is alone. This construction of maintaining separate elements in a unified whole is highly suggestive.

We are informed that Seurat made two comments about his intent in depicting the figures. He deprecated any significance attached to the individuals, stating, "I might just as well have painted the Horatii" (House 1980, 347). On another occasion, he said he wanted to do a modern version of the Pan-Athenaic Frieze of Phidias on the Parthenon. Is his attitude one of bemused irony? Is he satirizing the figures, ridiculing them because they have gotten all dressed up to do nothing on a Sunday afternoon? Or does he look upon them with a benign and indulgent attitude? It has been suggested that the two women on the far left—the one who fishes and the one beside her—are actually prostitutes. To fish means to fish for men or to sin, based on the similarity between the French word *(pêcher)* "to fish" and *(pécher)* "to sin." (Thomson 1985). Are we being encouraged to note the contrasts between the figures, the muscular boatman and the dandified man who sits behind him, elegant and in a top hat? Does his small size denote a quality of mockery? Is the overall schematization a statement on contemporary stiffness, rigidity, artifice, dehumanization, or the difficulty of forming significant interpersonal relations in the modern era?

If indeed this theme is present, certainly the formal emphasis on artistic harmony is of vital importance. The artist has carefully lined up the people, controlled their position, organized them, and eliminated their accidental appearance. Insofar as the artist's imposition of structure is so much a part of the painting, a suggestive theme of the painting is the synthetic function present in creativity (Kris [1933] 1952). The artist has created a scene that is orderly and weighted by an implacable presentation; the figures assume a puppetlike appearance because of their secondary importance. The artist, with great seriousness, had taken an impressionist theme of a leisurely outing and made twenty seven drawings, twenty seven panels, and three prior canvases to perfect the details and composition and to give the scene a stability and permanence.

It is of some interest that in the musical comedy by Stephen

Sondheim and James Lapine based on the painting, *Sunday in the Park with George* (1986), the composer and his librettist have emphasized the theme of artistic creativity. In the musical comedy, the lives of the characters are presented as entangled, petty, and mean-spirited. Their emotions are conflicted. Jealousy, envy, hostility, competition, and fear of abandonment threaten the scene with social disintegration. In the narrative, it is the artist's imposition of order and harmony upon the disorderly lives that stabilizes the figures into the final organized tableau of the painting, which terminates the first act of the play (Gordon 1992).

Although the painting under study is not autobiographical in the sense that the artist is depicted in it, it is of interest to turn to biographical material to see whether the work can be illuminated by some knowledge of Seurat's life. Seurat was described as a secretive, solitary man, extremely organized and compulsive in his actions (Broude 1978; Gedo 1989). He was born in 1859, the third of four siblings. A brother was born in 1863, when Georges was between three and four, and died in 1868. His father was a bailiff, who spent much of his time away from home, rejoining the family once a week for dinner. When Seurat left his home and set up his own studio, he returned to the family home on these occasions. His mother is described as "doting," and his father as "distant," somewhat of a religious fanatic, who often enacted a Mass celebration in the chapel he set up for himself, requiring his gardener to attend as a congregant. Early in his life, the father had an accident in which he had lost his left hand, and he wore a prosthesis. Seurat's secretiveness is evident in that for the last year and a half of his life he lived nearby with a mistress and had a child by her, but his family did not know of them. This secret was revealed only a day or two prior to his death when his mistress, his child, and he showed up at the parental home. He was already deathly ill with diphtheria. He died in 1891 at the age of thirty one.

Although it does seem strange that so much of Seurat's private life took place out of the awareness of his own family, it is not incompatible with Seurat's personality. He is considered by those who knew him to be prickly and touchy, easily offended and thus likely to assume a withdrawn and distant stance in his personal relationships. Artists who knew him were well aware of his sensitivity and his tendency to react with hurt pride in the face of slights or neglect. Nowhere is this better demonstrated than in his relationship with the critic Félix Fénéon. Fénéon was initially a great supporter of Seurat, and pointed out his merit in his sensitive description of *La Grande Jatte* when it was first exhibited in 1886. Fénéon, however, "needed an open dialogue with an artist in order to remain in tune with his work" (Halperin 1988, 131) Such was not easy to maintain with Seurat. After an initial meeting, which began in trust and friendship, there was a period of four years of increasing distrust and distance. In June 1890, Fénéon had written about Seurat's fellow neo-impressionist colleague, Paul Signac, praising him as an innovator and originator in the discovery of the neo-impressionist technique. Seurat, when he read Fénéon's comments, felt that he was disdainfully neglected in not having been mentioned at all, and he wrote an inarticulate letter to Fénéon in which his anger was barely controlled. A day or two later, Fénéon came to call on Seurat, and although Seurat was in his studio, he did not respond to Fénéon's ring. The uninvited intrusion by Fénéon threatened him with the exposure of his mistress and baby, whom he meant to keep secret from everyone. Seurat considered his studio to be violated by Fénéon, and responded to Fénéon's visit with another angry letter in which he stated, "I believe I have been wronged" (Halperin 1988, 142).

The two letters to Fénéon are unusual in that it was rare for Seurat to write anything. He maintained that Fénéon had denied Seurat's claims of "my earlier paternity" (Halperin 1988, 139)—

as the instigator of the technique of divisionism. Seurat initially expressed his gratitude to Fénéon, "You brought me out of eclipse," with the implication that subsequently he was let down, betrayed, and abandoned. Seurat felt as if Fénéon, by not giving him sufficient credit, had even denied his very existence. He wrote, "If I was unknown in 1885, I nonetheless existed, I and my vision" (Halperin 1988, 142). Fénéon was puzzled by the intensity of his reaction, which he felt was unjustified.

Félix Fénéon was a fascinating person in his own right, a great neo-impressionist critic, a man highly sensitive to the innovations that Seurat and his group were putting into effect. At the same time, Fénéon had a secretive second life as well; he was an active anarchist and arsonist. He was probably responsible for several bombings of Parisian sites which were part of the anarchist agenda. Although Fénéon was arrested, imprisoned and tried as an anarchist, charges could not be substantiated, and after a short prison sentence he was freed. After the personal tie with Seurat was broken, he maintained a tie with Seurat's work even after the painter's death. Seurat had sent Fénéon a study for his painting *Les Poseuses;* the critic became intensely attached to the work, had a black velvet cover made for it, and took it with him whenever he left Paris on business or vacation.

The relationship with Fénéon was one example of the difficulty Seurat experienced in personal relationships, and it adds significance to the fact that Seurat had kept the relationship with his mistress and baby a secret from his family and his friends. In fact, some of the language having to do with his relationship with Fénéon suggests a quality of libidinization. In Seurat's first letter to Fénéon, of June 20, 1890, he referred to Fénéon's comment that optical painting had "seduced—several young painters." Quite clearly, Seurat felt he should have been given credit for this "seduction" (Herbert et al. 1991, appendix 7, 383). He saw himself at a young age as the father of the movement rather than Signac. An undercurrent of unconscious homosexual attachment present in the relationship between Fénéon and Seurat is highly suggestive, and the need to avoid a more direct intimate personal contact in their relationship can be accounted for by the threat.

It is striking how much in the background women played in the neo-impressionist movement. Seurat's mistress, Madeleine Knoblock, does not emerge in the biographical accounts as having a character of her own. After his death, she maintained the view that she too had been badly treated by Seurat's former friends, and was not given the kind of recognition and regard to which she was due. Thus, she readily assumed an identity similar to his own, feeling betrayed and insufficiently regarded by others. Her complaint was hardly justified in that Seurat's parents were very generous in the allocation of Seurat's estate, permitting her to have a sizable portion of his work, which was divided subsequent to his death between her, Seurat's colleagues, and the family. Exactly two weeks after the death of the artist, on April 13, 1891, his young son also died, and was buried alongside his father in Père-Lachaise. Seurat's father died on May 24 of the same year. Seurat's mother died in 1899, leaving a life annuity to Seurat's mistress at the time of her death. Madeleine Knoblock died of cirrhosis of the liver in 1903.

Thus far—aside from the work of Mary M. Gedo (1989)—there has been little attempt to consider *La Grande Jatte* from a psychoanalytic perspective. Many of the critics and art historians who have approached the painting have done so with an emphasis on the social reality that Seurat was depicting. They suggest that Seurat was interested in pointing out the anomie which was part of contemporary society and which interfered with social cohesion. Timothy J. Clark, a prominent theorist who subscribes to this genre of criticism, has argued for an emphasis on the problem of social class (Clark 1984). An exclusive investment in the issue of social alienation and the critique of society as a chaotic and disjointed *mésalliance* leaves out of account the psychological dimensions which make the picture so evocative. Any tendency to see the human forms as stick figures and a puppetlike manifestation of this critique leaves out of account the emphasis on harmony, planning, and organization, which is so evident in the painting itself. Although many figures are unrelated, they are clearly grouped. Even the canoeist, who *seems* to be by himself, is actually made part of a threesome, and many of the other figures are paired. Relatedness is explicit throughout. The mother and little girl who walk toward us make the most direct contact with us. There is a familial grouping in the background, and there is a child in the pram in the right middle ground. In subject matter and visual vocabulary, there is an emphasis placed on family order. The technique of divisionism itself, the interest in keeping pigments separate and isolating the marks of the brush from one another, is compensated for by an emphasis on organization and a sense of synthesis of parts.

Many react to the picture as if it is a nostalgic evocation of a childhood scene long past, a memory of an outing on a Sunday afternoon with parents. The scene has a dreamlike quality, characterized by stillness and immobility, with only minor evocations of movement. The scene is one of play, leisure, and relaxation but is tinged with a note of ironic indulgence and detachment. No one is busy or at work, except perhaps the nurse—dressed, paradoxically, in the contemporary attire for a wet nurse—who accompanies the old lady sitting by the tree and the invisible artist, who has set the scene and is hidden from our view. In order to make this scene effective, division and splitting are necessary. In the artist's mind, there is a division between what the artist places on his canvas and what the eye forms in the mind. And in the presence of psychological fragmentation, a heavy emphasis on order becomes necessary. Pointillism is a technique which unites both separation and cohesiveness. It is likely that an artist, who has experienced with degrees of intensity the psychological developmental phases, is more likely to look for means to master the trauma associated with disjunction and opt for means that will overcome isolation and lead to harmony.

Lest we come to an easy explanation for the meaning of the painting and accept the view that artistic works can be fully described in verbal terms, let us note that Seurat leaves us with a puzzle. We are left with a feeling that the link between separateness and cohesion continues to be ambiguous. What is the meaning of the small triangle, which has no representational value, in the upper right-hand corner of the painting (ill. 4.2)? Does the artist leave us with a sense of his symbolic presence; is it simply an example of a geometric form meant to carry the quality of signature? Does the triangle represent the implicit presence of the artist, the markings of a brush which is best expressed by the intrusion of the organizing, containing frame which playfully intrudes?

It was of utmost importance for Seurat to believe that he had found a unique means for codifying and advancing the method of painting. Fénéon's lack of credit and recognition was a severe threat to what the painter had experienced as mastery in his method. Seurat's treatment of a rather frivolous and leisurelike activity with the emphasis a High Renaissance artist might have given to a theme of great weight, is an indication of how seriously he had taken the method itself. Thus, Seurat managed to create an art that confines itself not to the practical tasks of reality but to another order of being which replaces with organization and synthesis the potential threat of a disruptive reality.

We may well wonder from what roots the interest in order and harmony in the work of Seurat springs. Given his touchy, sensitive, and secretive nature and his tendency to experience

inarticulate mortification, his narcissistic withdrawal from colle-
giality and friendship, his distance and emotional separation, it
seems likely that a preoccupation with structure and composition in a work of art might well stem from a need for restitution
and recompense. An interest in reparation, the setting right and
recreation of an internally threatened world, might readily find
embodiment in a dedication to harmony, interrelationship, and
the fusion of color and light (Segal 1991). Indeed, a desperate
need to be acknowledged as the father of a newly created
method might serve further to cover over a fear of overwhelming
chaos and disorder.

Quite clearly, an analysis of *La Grande Jatte* from the point of
view of the personality of the artist leaves us with a sense of
falling short. Whatever inferences we may establish about the
personality, these are not represented directly in the work itself,
and biographical hints do little to heighten the aesthetic effect of
La Grande Jatte. This is not to say, however, that some artists,
particularly in the painting of self-portraits, are not able to bring
their own personality into the forefront of the work so that they
indeed contribute to the impact. Vincent van Gogh in his self-
portraits, which kept pace with shifts in his psychic state, gave
aesthetic content to changes as they occur in his personality, and
we respond to the work very much with his personality in mind
(see chapter 1). This is particularly true of Rembrandt's self-
portraits, as I shall demonstrate in chapter 5. We would be hard
pressed to say this, however, about the felt presence of Seurat,
and in fact, if my inference about the upper right-hand corner is
correct, he has "geometricized" and impersonalized his presence
and removed its human quality.

In order to arrive at a psychoanalytic view of the means by
which the theme of separation and cohesion achieves an aesthetic effect we do well to examine the means of representation,
the primary process modes of establishing relations Freud de-

4.2 Georges Seurat, *Un Dimanche à la Grande Jatte,* (detail) (Chicago: The
Art Institute of Chicago). Courtesy of The Art Institute of Chicago.

scribed in *The Interpretation of Dreams* (1900). Such a mode of approach is particularly apt in an analysis of *La Grande Jatte*. In this work, we are specifically concerned with relations of colors to one another, of light, of masses, of figures, of surface to depth, and of movement to immobility. In fact, Seurat's careful planning of the work itself is an indication how concerned he was with the establishment of related elements in a harmonious whole.

In works of art in which narrative content is clear-cut because of the presence of literary sources, we have a component which allows us to understand specific relations between figures in a scene. In *La Grande Jatte* such literary references, of course, are absent. To this extent, *La Grande Jatte* approaches the manifest content of a dream in which secondary revision or the capacity for conscious fantasy has played a minimal role, thus allowing separate and isolated fragments to carry a weight on their own.

The familiar mechanisms of displacement and condensation utilized in the dream work are suggested by the criticism which the work has evoked. Varying interpretations have been offered for the standing couple on the right, the reduced size for the man with the cane on the left, and as has been previously mentioned, for the woman who fishes. Reference has been made to the monkey as a condensation for the artist, who "apes" nature. And the overall chromatic and pointillist emphasis is a manifestation for the secondary revision which pulls the disparate elements together.

Regarding the establishment of relations between elements in the dream thoughts, Freud pointed out that there is little opportunity for the visual representation of logical relationships such as contiguity, connection, and the sharing of common elements. Freud turned to the visual artist at this point to demonstrate how the painter uses a technique similar to the dreamer. He pointed out that when Raphael wanted to make a statement relevant to philosophy or to poetry, he disregarded the factor of simultaneity in time. In Raphael's *School of Athens* and *Parnassus*, he groups philosophers and poets from various epochs. Thus, a connection in thought is established through visual groupings. Seurat does something similar. He groups the man and the woman in the right foreground, and they are definitely related to one another through their physical contact. The three figures in the left foreground, however, are left ambiguous. Are they related to one another or unrelated? It is not clear, and thus the issue of whether they are separated or connected is left up in the air. Although the right foreground and the left foreground figures seem to be unconnected as groups, Seurat uses the dog in the foreground to depict a movement from one group to the other and thus forms a connection via displacement where it is lacking in terms of human contact. Over and over again, we are left unclear as to whether the relations of the figurative objects are connected or separated, interactive or alienated. Are the two soldiers in the left background indeed reacting to the man with the trumpet? Is the girl running toward the three figures sitting in the right middle ground? The only time we have a threesome which does establish a psychological bond is that between the presumptive mother, infant, and father in the middle background.

How are we to think of Seurat's association of *La Grande Jatte* to the *Horatii* and the Panathenaic frieze? He was clearly considering groupings which fulfill a particular purpose, and the classical references indicate the ambition he had in mind. He was also referring to groups formed for revolutionary purposes and a major religious procession (Gedo 1989). In both cases, he emphasized the purposive and cohesive aspect in the figures and his sense that they belong together. The emphasis on harmony—Seurat's primary conception of art—cuts across isolation of parts to establish a unified totality.

SUMMARY

Much of the aesthetic and psychological impact of *La Grande Jatte* can be understood as a dialogue of cohesion and separation. The splitting of the marks of the brush and the colors, the breaking up of the colors, the pointillist technique, as well as the isolation of the figures from one another, heightens the sense of separation. Order is reimposed upon this fragmentation by the deliberate composition, by the expectation that the eye will unify the disparity, and the marked attention to the surface and the emphatically painted frame, which leaves no doubt that finally everything is contained and in its proper place. The separate parts have been unified into one cohesive space.

REFERENCES

Broude, N., ed. 1978. *Seurat in Perspective*. Englewood Cliffs, N.J.: Prentice Hall.

Clark, T. J. 1984. *The Painting of Modern Life: Paris in the Art of Manet and His Followers*. New York: Alfred A. Knopf.

Freud, S. 1900. *The Interpretation of Dreams. Standard Edition* 4 and 5. London: Hogarth Press.

Gedo, M. M. 1989. The *Grande Jatte* as the icon of a new religion: A psycho-iconographic interpretation. *Museum Studies* (Art Institute of Chicago) 14:223–37.

Gordon, J. 1992. *Art Isn't Easy: The Theater of Stephen Sondheim*. New York: Da Capo Press.

Halperin, J. U. 1988. *Félix Fénéon: Aesthete and Anarchist in Fin-de-Siècle Paris*. New Haven: Yale University Press.

Herbert, R. L., F. Cachin, A. Distel, S. A. Stein, and G. Tinterow. 1991. *Georges Seurat*. New York: Harry N. Abrams.

House, J. 1980. Meaning in Seurat's figure paintings. *Art History* 3:345–56.

Kris, E. [1933] 1952. *Psychoanalytic Explorations in Art*. New York: International Universities Press.

Nochlin, L. 1989. Seurat's *Grande Jatte:* An anti-utopian allegory. *Museum Studies* (Art Institute of Chicago) 14:133–53.

Pope-Hennessy, J. 1991. *Learning to Look.* New York: Doubleday.

Segal, H. 1991. *Dream, Phantasy, and Art.* London: New Library of Psychoanalysis, Tavistock/Routledge.

Sondheim, S. and J. Lapine. 1986. *Sunday in the Park with George.* New York: Dodd, Mead.

Thomson, R. 1985. *Seurat.* Oxford: Phaidon.

{ *Five* }

REMBRANDT

and Two Self-Portraits

FRICK AND KENWOOD HOUSE

*It is a widely acknowledged truth that an artist who takes up self-*portraiture is engaged in a quasi-psychoanalytic task, in terms of defining, using, distorting, or discovering the self. How much more so is this in the case of Rembrandt van Rijn, who painted, etched, or drew himself at least seventy five times in a variety of developmental phases, almost from the beginning of his career as an artist to the end. Manifestly, the task involves visual self-examination, standing in front of a mirror, reading one's features, and recording what one sees. From a psychoanalytic point of view, it is important to discern the factors contributing to the artist's devotion to the task, the motives which set it into action, the product itself, and the impact on the viewer of such self-preoccupation.

This chapter will consider the self-portrait within a psychoanalytic context, focusing on the significance of the mirror, and will examine the experience of self-observation and mirroring as a developmental phase. I shall then examine the self-portrait in the life and work of Rembrandt, concentrating on the Frick self-portrait of 1658 and the self-portrait at Kenwood House (ills. 5.1 and 5.2, respectively). I shall discuss self-portraiture in terms of current views of the psychology of the self and the self as both a changing and enduring psychological entity. The chapter will close with a discussion of self-analysis in a generic sense, as a visual and psychological experience, and the correlation between the two.

The theme of self-portraiture has not escaped the examination of art critics and art historians. This is particularly true about Rembrandt's self-portraits. Two recent studies (Wright 1982; Chapman 1990) have examined Rembrandt's work in this area primarily from an art historical point of view. Christopher Wright's book is mainly a picture book, and has little psychological value.[1] H. P. Chapman's work has greater psychological depth, and more will be said about it later.

The theme of self-portraiture as a genre does not have a lengthy past history. Joseph Leo Koerner (1993) credits Albrecht Dürer with the oldest true artist's portrait, at least in the North, toward the end of the fifteenth century. Erwin Panofsky (1955) also gives Dürer the credit, and credits the 1498 Dürer painting in the Prado as "the first independent self-portrait ever produced" (42). There is some question about the Dürer priority, and some have claimed that Jan van Eyck's *Man in the Red Turban*, painted in 1433 and now in the National Gallery in London, is probably a self-portrait. It also has been suggested that the French painter Jean Fouquet produced a likeness of himself in 1450. In any case, it is the fifteenth century which is seen as crucial in the development of this genre. Historians generally have credited the development of this interest to the Renaissance concern with individuality, autonomy, and the study of man as a unique and self-contained being. It is of

1. Wright suggests, "It may well be that many of [the] self-portraits were demonstrations of his abilities, displayed in order to impress prospective patrons; a kind of showing-off which has nothing to do with self-analysis" (1982, 26). Wright does not address why a self-portrait might be a better display of his abilities than any other representation, particularly in view of the fact that Rembrandt was no great beauty and the portraits do not flatter.

interest that antiquity provides us with no artifacts or literary texts indicating that self-portraiture existed. Thus it is all the more striking that Rembrandt was preoccupied with a means of expression that did not have a long art historical tradition.

In tracing the evolution of this preoccupation in Rembrandt, one can discern a variety of motives which led to the artist's interest. Initially, particularly in the small etchings which characterized his early attempts at self-portraiture, Rembrandt was interested in representing particular emotions and their impact on facial expression. He studied his face in the mirror in order to determine how emotional expressiveness could be depicted. In many of these early works, the eyes were shaded, a representation associated with seventeenth-century conceptions of melancholia and inwardness. Although this kind of depiction is a form of self-scrutiny, one can hardly call these early examples of grimacing attempts to delineate psychological states of any depth.

As Rembrandt progressed in his self-depiction, he assumed a number of guises which were in keeping with his conception of a successful artistic career. Early, he portrayed himself in military gear, at other times wearing a beret and a chain. Chapman (1990) points out that the beret was often associated with the guise of a learned painter, and a golden chain around the neck was a sign of favor granted by a king or a prince and was occasionally given to artists whom royalty deemed worthy. Although Rembrandt did not achieve such recognition from royalty, he did not hesitate to give himself this status in his self-portraits. In this regard, he emulated Peter Paul Rubens. Rubens was an artist who did assume an aristocratic bearing, and was recognized by royal patrons as worthy of such elevation. In Rembrandt's situation, his "nobility" was not a reflection of an achieved social status but was more a sign of an imitative fiction.

It is possible that events in the life of the artist account for shifts in the number and style of Rembrandt's self-portraits. There was a decrease in the number of self-portraits in the early 1640s, and this was period fraught with stress and tragedy in the life of the artist. In his biography of Rembrandt, Jakob Rosenberg (1964) refers to this period as a time of emotional crisis. The artist's wife, Saskia, died in 1642. A few years later, he had an affair with a housemaid, Geertge Dircx. She had been his son Titus's nursemaid, and she brought a series of lawsuits against him, maintaining that he had offered her marriage. By 1649, he was instrumental in having her committed to an institution, and had started another affair with a new companion, Hendrickje Stoffels (Schwartz 1985). In addition, his financial situation had deteriorated to the point that his possessions were sold to pay off his creditors and avoid bankruptcy.

The Frick self-portrait of 1658 (ill. 5.1) is distinguished by its majestic frontality. Rembrandt treats the chair in which he sits as if it is a throne. His gaze is direct and intense. Although his face is tired and lined with care, the entire gaze gives an impression of stoicism and grandeur. He wears a long tunic, and holds in his hand a knobbed maulstick as if it were a scepter. There is a strong emphasis on rough brush strokes, with colors especially favored by the Venetians, particularly Titian. The limited colors of yellow and red and gold and black continue a tradition favored by the ancient court painter to Alexander, Apelles. For painters concerned with ennobling the craft of painting and elevating their own status, the link with Apelles is critical.

Rembrandt's need to establish connections with Rubens and Titian through signs of royal favor can be understood as an interest in augmenting his identity as a supreme artist. However, the identity is also subverted since Rembrandt could not, in reality, conceive of himself as an artist to a court. In fact, Rembrandt's intent was much more likely to be ironic and to be disparaging of an artist who was interested in inflating his own

5.1 Rembrandt van Rijn, *Self Portrait* (New York: The Frick Collection). Copyright The Frick Collection, New York.

status. The borrowing in this instance is probably a veiled form of disparagement and criticism rather than a means of attaining status honoring a fellow artist.[2]

It probably was not until the early to mid-1660s that Rembrandt painted his first portrait as a painter, the Kenwood self-portrait (ill. 5.2). Rembrandt appears as a dignified working artist engaged in the act of painting, addressing an easel, holding his palette, and backgrounded by two concentric circles vaguely suggestive of maps of a nonspecific universality.

There is particular significance to the fact that the Frick portrait comes at a nadir in Rembrandt's life, yet the portrait manifestly suggests nothing of this. The portrait communicates an exaggerated and grandiose majesty, the depiction of a mastery in his art at a time when fortune and reality had dealt him heavy blows. Yet it is hardly conceivable that defensive needs alone would propel him to such powerful heights of creativity. It is likely that the artist was already engaged in a process of self-examination and introspection which made the outward circumstances of his life less compelling and overwhelming. Thus we may consider the lengthy and repeated experience of visual self-

---

2. The art historical enterprise of tracing sources for a particular artist's work must account for the psychological significance of a particular ancestor in the experience of the artist. Wollheim (1987) has pointed out how borrowing generates fresh meaning in a work and how often an artist's visual source does not merely reflect the stylistic addition but also adds a particular meaning. He pointed out how Poussin, in borrowing from Titian, was making a statement about the presence of desire in a classical context. By borrowing from a Pietà for a mythological subject, he raised the power of a pagan myth by adding a sense of Christian mystery. Freud, in his paper "Great is Diana of the Ephesians" (1912), also indicated that borrowing can heighten the value of an object. Freud borrowed his title from Goethe, and in doing so established the importance of standing on the shoulders of a revered ancestor. In the paper, he traces a chronology from the Greek goddess, Oupis, to Artemis to the Virgin Mary, thus establishing that there is a need to refind the image of a powerful idealized maternal figure who is also a virgin. Each trace from the past adds an attribute to the present-day object.

5.2 Rembrandt van Rijn, *Self Portrait* (London: Kenwood House, The Iveagh Bequest).

examination a movement toward insight and a form of self-analysis.

The experience of looking at oneself in the mirror has been the subject of extensive psychoanalytic work. Beginning with Freud's 1914 paper on narcissism, the myth of Narcissus has had an appeal for the psychoanalyst and has been considered as paradigmatic of early stages of development. Other psychoanalysts—Leonard Shengold (1974), Jacques Lacan (1977, 1978)—have also found the psychological experience associated with the mirror to have profound psychological meaning. In its regressive form, narcissistic preoccupation is a perversion in which self-examination takes on a libidinal quality and becomes a replacement for an interest in objects which were previously the aim of externally directed sexual drives. The young infant, prior to the development of an investment in external reality, expends much of its interests on the archaic self and the body, inner sensations, and hallucinatory gratifications when faced with frustration. With further development, these interests become directed outward but never to such a complete extent that investment in the self is totally given up, and never to such a extent that the self no longer preserves an interest in its own integration, cohesiveness, and strength (Kohut 1971).

Insofar as the making of a self-portrait often requires the actual experience of looking at oneself in a mirror, this activity is manifestly narcissistic. But with the passing of infantile stages, the observation of oneself in a mirror takes on additional meanings and complexities which are not present in the first stages of life. As Freud (1914) indicated, narcissistic preoccupation with the self can be understood on a number of different levels. One can see oneself in terms of who one was, who one thinks one actually is, whom one repudiates, or who one would like to be. Ludwig Goldscheider (1937), in his review of five hundred self-portraits, gives examples of each. The most common example is the idealized version of the self, the artist depicting himself in terms of whom he would like to be. However, this is by no means the only type. The artist prior to antiquity, as in Egyptian reliefs or medieval sculpture, although not offering a veridical mirror image, might depict himself generically as working away at his trade in the midst of others, as a background figure in a religious tableau, or later as a worshiping follower and participant in Christ's passion, as Rembrandt did early in his career.[3]

With the development of the northern European and Italian Renaissance, the artist began not only to include himself as a member of a group but to single himself out as worthy of individual depiction. And it is with the Renaissance that we begin to have views of the artists as subjects deserving independent status.

I have observed that Koerner (1993) found a Dürer self-portrait at the end of the fifteenth century critical in the attention the artist diverted to his own depiction, and he recognized this as a pivotal moment in northern European art. Among the greatest self-portraitists, we shortly find Titian, particularly in old age, depicting himself in the garb of working artist and Rubens, who emphasized his courtly and worldly status, shortly thereafter. Rembrandt borrowed from both, and depicted himself as both worldly and courtly.

When we come to the Frick self-portrait, we see an amalgamation of the two tendencies combined with a new element. Rembrandt saw himself as a working artist who belonged to a particular kind of tradition, and the tradition was expressed in the high status that was granted to the working artist. As pointed out in chapter 2, Velázquez, closely allied in time, was similarly depicting himself in *Las Meninas*. However, Rembrandt added a component not present in Titian, Rubens, or Velázquez; this was

3. Edvard Munch, among others, depicted a repudiated and shunned self.

the presence of an introspective psychological component. In the Frick portrait, we are made aware, through the posture of the figure and the piercing intensity of the facial expression, of a conflicted psychological state. We are made conscious of an artist in the process of depicting himself at work and simultaneously fictionalizing his presence through his attire and posture.

The artist is engaged in a double task, self-observation and execution. The artist is observing his own reflection in a mirror, and almost simultaneously he is attempting to render this self-observation through his art. He both observes and acts, and in doing so must reflect, on a conscious or unconscious level, on the means by which he is to render his image. On a conscious level, he makes decisions about which aspects of his features to emphasize and which to submerge in importance. In an artist like Rembrandt, capable of a psychological dimension, there is an inevitable tendency to find in his features not simply the depiction of a physical sign but also to include some aspect of his life experience. The making of the portrait then becomes a striving for representation and a process evocative of past experiences of analytic self-regard. A perceived reality is filtered through a life of experience previously recorded through a series of self-portraits of which each in the series is a further delineation of some aspect of the self.

As a result of the depiction, the artist makes room for the viewer's presence. This quality of "otherness" is also to be thought of as present within the portrait. Just as *Las Meninas* had made a place for the viewer, through its spatial structure and glances of the figures, the self-portrait, through position and gaze, creates a point of view for an observer, and places the viewer in a relationship to the observed object.

In the Frick self-portrait, this positioning is brought about by the quality of ambiguity associated with gaze of the subject. The Frick portrait belongs to the group of Rembrandt's self-portraits in which the viewer is present as observer and thus someone who is also included in the work. The encircling gestures of the arms have an enveloping and embracing quality. The verticality of the figure and the magisterial gaze place the observer in a somewhat lower and subservient position. Simultaneously, we are observing a figure preoccupied with inner thoughts. For this reason, it is much easier to relate the Frick self-portrait to the realities of Rembrandt's misfortunes: social ostracism, personal losses, and the shift in his artistic status. Observers readily can see in the Frick portrait an attempt to establish a regal and commanding bearing when grounds for such were lacking in reality, a need to deny a depressive quality by hyperbolizing an experience of mastery which would elevate him above the distress of his real condition.

Such a compensatory referent does not accompany the Kenwood self-portrait (ill. 5.2). Here, the magisterial quality is lacking, and Rembrandt has depicted himself altogether in the role of the working painter with a canvas nearby. Although austere and dignified, the portrait lacks the quality of defiance and protest present in the Frick. In fact, the viewer at this point is not embraced but somewhat rebuffed, set apart perhaps by a blob of red paint on the tip of his nose, and made aware of the fact that this is a man who has now attained a quality of independence and serenity beyond the need to deny hardship and suffering. Here, there is a stirring balance of the connection between self-observation and execution. By minimizing the representational elements in the lower part of the painting, the portrait recognizes the special tension between representation of self as artist and the means by which he achieves his effect, the presence and use of simple and unmodulated paint without the enabling fiction of the Frick dress-up.

The special quality associated with self-observation and the activity of its depiction is caught in both the Frick and the Kenwood paintings. There is a highlighting of the painterly qualities associated with the hands of the artist. Although this is not atypical in much portrait work, where there is likely to be an emphasis placed on the facial features, in Rembrandt this seems to be particularly important, given prominence beyond conventional ways of painting. Mieke Bal (1991) has made a particular point about the looseness of the fingers holding the maulstick in the Frick portrait. In her reading of this painting, she emphasizes the component of absence in the gesture, and suggests that the gap between the first and second fingers symbolizes a lack equivalent to castration. She points out that in the Kenwood House painting, in contrast to the Frick, the fingers cannot be discerned to hold anything. In fact, they are hardly represented. Bal suggests that gap in the fingers in the Frick, in contrast to the area between the index finger and the thumb, which is occupied by the maulstick, in its emptiness represents failure or unease. Perhaps it is only in the periphery of the representation of this gesture that we discern something of the backgrounded psychic reality which Rembrandt had experienced. The resolve in the face is subverted by the emptiness of the gap in the lower part.

Bal's formulation is based on the Lacanian attention given to the experience of self-mirroring, which finds so prominent a position in the thought of Lacan of an imaginary phase. Lacan (1977), suggests that the mirror view of the young infant, which leads to a spurious sense of totality, has an ominous and threatening aspect associated with it. Between the ages of six and eighteen months, the infant must overpower the initial threat and move toward the potential growth of its ego and the antecedents for somatic and psychological cohesion.

Lacanian notions of the importance of the mirror phase are suggestive in a discussion of self-portraiture. Lacan recognized the unsurmounted mirror phase as leading to the possibility of psychological fragmentation. The infant confronted by a mirror image not only sees itself by reflection and recognizes the similarities between movement and the mirror image and movement in its own self but also recognizes the possibility of being divided; the self exists not only in terms of a subjective state but also in terms of an objective visual image. Thus, here too, the threat of division and fragmentation exists. Since it is literally impossible to depict oneself without at the same time engaging in a distortion, the artist can do nothing other than confront the potential alienation of the self which is present in such distortion. The inevitable distortion is dependent on the fact that the mirror image is reversed. Right is left, and left is right. Any movement in the mirror which is meant to correct the reversal has to take account of this paradox.

The two Rembrandt self-portraits under discussion are understood in psychoanalytic terms as representations for current trends in self psychology, which place the self and narcissistic issues in the center of our discourse (Kohut 1971). The Rembrandt self-portraits explore the experience of mirroring, its relationship to a sense of the "other," and the simultaneous experience of looking and being observed. Early mirroring leads to transformations of narcissism and transmutations in the direction of creativity and a mature acceptance of reality (Kohut 1966). In depicting himself at critical stages in his own life, when he was overwhelmed by psychological stress and suffering, Rembrandt was able to transform these experiences into heroic defiance, self-observation, resolution, and serenity. Thus, he established a harmonious balance between the experience of adversity, the depiction of the experience, and the representation of the self as first bowed then surmounting and later enduring. This is the progression we note from the Frick to the Kenwood self-portraits.

SUMMARY

The experience of the artist who observes himself in a mirror while engaged in self-portraiture is examined from the point of view of a contemporary psychoanalytic perspective regarding mirroring. The experience is critical in the thinking of Lacan and the emphasis he places upon the mirror in the development of the imaginary stage as well as in the work of Kohut, who describes an essential aspect in early development in terms of the empathic mirroring of the child by the parent. In the case of Rembrandt, it is suggested that the preoccupation with self-portraiture fulfilled a quasi-self-analytic task, enabling the artist through visual observation to arrive at self-understanding; thus the portraits document a progression from an overcompensatory reaction to stress to a state of acceptance.

REFERENCES

Bal, M. 1991. Reading *"Rembrandt."* Cambridge: Cambridge University Press.

Chapman, H. P. 1990. *Rembrandt Self-Portraits.* Princeton: Princeton University Press.

Freud, S. 1912. Great is Diana of the Ephesians. *Standard Edition* 12:342–44. London: Hogarth Press.

———. 1914. On narcissism. *Standard Edition* 14:73–102. London: Hogarth Press.

Goldscheider, L. 1937. *Five Hundred Self-Portraits.* London: George Allen and Unwin.

Koerner, J. L. 1993. *The Moment of Self-Portraiture in German Renaissance Art.* Chicago: University of Chicago Press.

Kohut, H. 1966. Forms and transformations of narcissism. *J. Am. Psychoanal. Assoc.* 14:243–72.

———. 1971. *The Analysis of Self.* New York: International Universities Press.

Lacan, J. 1977. *Écrits*. New York: W. W. Norton.

———. 1978. *The Four Fundamental Concepts of Psychoanalysis*. New York: W. W. Norton.

Panofsky, E. 1955. *Albrecht Dürer*. Princeton: Princeton University Press.

Rosenberg, J. 1964. *Rembrandt: Life and Work*. London: Phaidon Press.

Schwartz, G. 1985. *Rembrandt: His Life, His Paintings*. New York: Viking Press.

Shengold, L. 1974. The metaphor of the mirror. *J. Am. Psychoanal. Assoc.* 22:97–115.

Wollheim, R. 1987. *Painting As an Art*. Princeton: Princeton University Press.

Wright, C. 1982. *Rembrandt: Self-Portraits*. New York: Viking Press.

Six

L'AVVENTURA AND THE

Presentation of Emptiness

It may be the special attribute of the masterpiece that the nature of its reception carries over something of its own message. For several decades Michelangelo Antonioni's *L'avventura* was declared, according to the authoritative poll conducted by *Sight and Sound*, a masterpiece, often designated as the second-best film of all time, following *Citizen Kane*. In the poll of 1992, *L'avventura* no longer appears. Perhaps critics and directors have become bored with it. If this indeed were the case, *L'avventura* has fulfilled itself admirably. It has become a lost masterpiece—a film which could not sustain itself, now dismissed and discharged because of inattention—a central theme of the work itself.

The film concerns itself with the themes of emptiness and the difficulty of forming committed attachments in the face of a world characterized by impermanence and decline. A psychoanalytic perspective is pertinent in that the theme, while ostensibly describing the failure of an era, is in fact an intrapsychic concern projected as a social imperative. In this chapter, the techniques of the filmmaker are considered as creative modes for depicting projective intrapsychic states.

L'avventura was made by Antonioni in 1959, and released in 1960. The story opens with Anna, a twenty five-year-old, dark-

6.1 Michelangelo Antonioni's *L'avventura*. Courtesy of The Museum of Modern Art / Film Stills Archive.

haired woman, who tells her father that she is leaving on a cruise for a few days. He is a wealthy retired diplomat, who is depressed about her departure, and he strives to make her feel guilty because in leaving she abandons him. He also tells her that her fiancé, Sandro, is not a reliable person and that he will never marry her. We find out later that Sandro, a man of about thirty five, works as an estimator for a contractor and is also well off. Sandro and Anna had been separated for about a month, and Anna is on her way, with her blonde friend, Claudia, to meet Sandro at his apartment prior to the cruise. When they arrive at his building, Anna leaves Claudia waiting while she goes up to his apartment to fetch him. Her attitude toward him is ambiguous. On the one hand, she seems reluctant to meet with him, looks at him quizzically, and without saying much, removes her dress, and they make love while Claudia waits outside. Claudia listlessly enters an art gallery while she is waiting. When Anna and Sandro are through with lovemaking, the three quickly drive off to the yacht.

The cruise takes place off the Aeolian Islands, on the north coast of Sicily. A number of other people accompany the three on the yacht, which belongs to a married friend, Patrizia. She is accompanied by her lover Raimondo. There is another couple: a young woman, Giulia, who has a relationship with Corrado, an older man, who criticizes Giulia bitterly, ridicules her and continually embarrasses her by pointing out her deficiencies. Giulia takes these barbs passively, without expressing any overt hostile feelings to Corrado.

Anna, in spite of maintaining a physical relationship with Sandro, is restless and self-preoccupied. She suddenly decides that she wants to dive overboard for a swim, and when she is in the water, she screams that she sees a shark. She is rescued from the danger by Sandro, who jumps in after her. But once Anna and Claudia are in their cabin and changing out of their swim suits, Anna says that she made up the shark story, but offers no explanation for her deceit. Instead, she impulsively gives Claudia a blouse which Claudia admires.

When the members of the cruising party go ashore to explore a desolate island, Patrizia and Raimondo stay behind while Patrizia listlessly works on a jigsaw puzzle. Raimondo tries to interest her in lovemaking, but she is bored with his advances, and she gratifies his fetishistic interests by allowing him to admire her shoe and foot. On the deserted island, Corrado and

Claudia look at ancient ruins while Corrado ignores his wife, Giulia, whom he continues to depreciate. When Anna and Sandro go off by themselves, Anna is obviously unhappy, dissatisfied with Sandro, and tells him that she wants to have time by herself. When he cannot convince her of his love, he retreats and goes to sleep, and Anna appears to wander off.

When the weather begins to change and a storm threatens, the party is told that they must leave, and they then discover that they cannot find Anna. Sandro, Claudia, Corrado, and Giulia spend much time looking for her, but they find no sign of her. Sandro and Corrado find a single shack which is boarded up. They break down the door, and find that it belongs to a lonely fisherman who lives there, but Anna is not in there either. Sandro, Claudia, and Corrado stay overnight in the cabin. The next day, although Sandro seems serious about the search, he shows little feeling of loss or much emotion. It soon becomes obvious that Claudia and Sandro are drawn to each other. Claudia is obviously the one who is most upset about the loss of her friend. Initially, she blames Sandro for Anna's disappearance, but as time passes their mutual attraction becomes heightened.

As the search for Anna continues, the searchers become distracted. They find an ancient vase on the island, and become interested in that. Anna's father arrives by hydrofoil, and Claudia gives him the two books that Anna had with her before she disappeared. One is F. Scott Fitzgerald's novel *Tender Is the Night;* the other is a Bible, which her father takes as a sign that she could not have suicided. He is visibly shaken when he notices that Claudia has put on the blouse which Anna had previously given her because she had become wet in the rainstorm, and Claudia is obviously distressed to see his reaction, as though he considers that she is somehow implicated in Anna's disappearance.

Sandro and Claudia then part. He decides to continue the

search in one direction, following some men who have been arrested because of smuggling, suspecting that they may know something about Anna's fate. Claudia decides to visit other islands to look for Anna by herself. In parting, Claudia and Sandro kiss passionately, but she is troubled by her attraction to her friend's lover so shortly after the loss of her friend.

Sandro watches the smugglers being interviewed by the police, but they apparently know nothing about Anna's disappearance. He finds Claudia as she is waiting for a train. In spite of her disclaimers and anxiety about their growing relationship, he follows her on the train, but leaves on her insistence. He then looks for the writer of a newspaper article, who suggests that he has some additional information about Anna's disappearance that he can share. When Sandro arrives in the town, Messina, to consult the columnist, he finds himself in the midst of a publicity stunt caused by a young, attractive woman, Gloria Perkins, who creates a spectacle in order to draw attention to herself.

After a search on other islands, Claudia appears at the villa where Patrizia lives with her husband, Ettore. Ettore is Sandro's employer and the man who pays Sandro a high salary for his estimates on proposed construction sites. Also present are the unhappy couple, Giulia and Corrado. Giulia is attracted to a young artist, Goffredo, who invites Giulia to his studio to see his art. Giulia invites Claudia to accompany her, but when Goffredo kisses Giulia, she easily succumbs and asks Claudia to leave. Giulia is clearly taking her vengeance on Corrado by yielding to the young man.

Claudia then joins Sandro as he ostensibly continues his search for Anna. Sandro had been informed by the journalist that a pharmacist might have seen Anna in the town of Troina, and when he questions him, he finds that a woman who might be Anna may have left on a bus to Noto, another town nearby. The pharmacist whom Sandro meets has been married for three months, and is engaged in a quarrelsome relationship with his wife, who depreciates him much in the way that Corrado depreciates Giulia. She accuses him of infidelity. When he tries to escape from her, she follows him out of the store, and continues to harangue him. In fact, a particular point is made of the shortness of their relationship, and how unpleasant it has become in such a brief period of time.

Sandro and Claudia together drive to Noto, pass through a modern architectural site which is empty, and they see no one. Claudia states that the place reminds her of a cemetery. They then make passionate love in a field near the town, consummating their relationship. When they arrive at Noto, Sandro and Claudia separate. He goes into the hotel in order to discover whether Anna is there. Claudia is left alone in the midst of a large crowd of silent men who examine her in a hostile and provocative manner. She is anxious about the prospect of Sandro finding Anna in the hotel, and she is anxious about the crowd of hostile, leering men outside. They spend the day in Noto, ascend a church tower to view the beautiful piazza, and Sandro tells Claudia he is considering returning to architecture, for which he was trained, rather than continuing with his lucrative but meaningless life as an estimator. Sandro then leaves Claudia to visit a museum, which is closed. As he wanders through the square, he notices a young architectural student who has sketched a detail of a neighboring church. While examining the sketch, Sandro dangles his key chain over it and inadvertently knocks over an inkwell which destroys a beautiful drawing of a building detail. Although the scene is done without dialogue, we are made aware of Sandro's envy of the young architectural student and his fine drawing as well as Sandro's failed ambitions and his inability to fulfill his earlier goals. When he returns to Claudia, he approaches her sexually with some violence, which she recognizes as being reactive to some other situation and thus not based on loving feeling toward her.

Next, Sandro and Claudia arrive at the luxurious San Domenico Palace Hotel in Taormina, where Ettore and Patrizia have gathered together a large party. Claudia is tired from their travels, and as Sandro prepares to join the party, Claudia says that she prefers not to join the others, and she goes to bed alone. When Sandro descends to the gathering, he is restless and listless. He notices that Gloria Perkins, the young woman who was the center of attention in Messina, is present at the party, and she is attracted to him.

When Claudia arises in the early morning and finds that Sandro is not in his room, she checks with Patrizia and Ettore, who do not know where he is. She runs through the hotel looking for him. Suddenly she comes upon him lying on a couch with the half-dressed Gloria Perkins, with whom he has been having a sexual encounter. Sandro is overcome with shame when he sees that Claudia has discovered his infidelity. As he flees, Gloria Perkins asks him for money "as a souvenir." When Claudia runs out of the hotel, Sandro follows her. He sits on a bench near where she stands silently; he is mortified and guilt-ridden because of his behavior. Claudia approaches him and raises her hand behind his head in an uncertain gesture which finally ends in a caress of forgiveness. The film ends with a view of Mount Etna in the distance.

When we examine the film through a psychological lens, we note that it uses the search for Anna as an allegorical quest for fulfillment (Lesser 1964). On the surface, the characters are concerned with the fate of Anna, and yet as the film moves along, the protagonists and the viewers forget about this search and become preoccupied with other matters. Such displacement of interest is well depicted by Antonioni himself, who said shortly after the film was completed that he was frequently asked what happened to Anna. He replied, "Somebody told me that she committed suicide, but I don't believe it" (Samuels 1970, 10). Antonioni, in the fashioning of the film, had to work against the advice of producers who wanted her fate to be explicit and defined in the narrative. It was suggested that the plot should include an addition that she had suicided or that she would reappear in the last part of the film, in the party at San Domenico. Antonioni strenuously resisted such advice. It was his point that her fate was of a secondary nature; the search itself is what gave meaning to his film.

Insofar as the film reflects a contemporary preoccupation, the theme concerns the difficulties present in forming loving and committed relationships in the modern world. The requirements of modern life, adaptation to reality, particularly in the economic sphere, and the need to maintain a psychological identity in such a sphere can no longer sustain the freedom of communication and the ability to invest one's emotional ties in permanent relationships. A world characterized by impermanence, commercialism, and spiritual vacuity which leads to despair has drained the capacity of modern man to sustain meaningful values.

The film begins with Anna's inability to free herself from her parental attachment. Although she chooses to leave her father in order to go on a cruise with her lover, she does so with a sense of desperation and unhappy sulkiness. Even when she engages in physical love, there is little fulfillment and she does so with partially hostile intent directed toward her friend Claudia, whom she causes to wait for her. Her sense of impermanence is such that she half expects that her friend is already standing in the wings waiting to take her lover away from her.

Throughout the film, Claudia stands as an observer of others, who are engaged in sexual relationships. She witnesses Anna and Sandro making love at the beginning. On the yacht, she watches Patrizia and Raimondo engage in their perverse fetishistic relationship. Toward the middle of the film, she sees Giulia and the teenager, who are about to make love, and at the end she finds Sandro and Gloria Perkins in a liaison as well. None of these relationships is fulfilling. All of the relationships are characterized by degradation, betrayal, despair, hostility, and lack of satisfaction.

Claudia can readily observe how difficult it is to find a fulfilling object and how often in the face of a lost original object, one must seek a series of surrogate objects, none of whom gives satisfaction (Freud 1912). In the film, sexuality is used as an antidote to despair and a way of dealing with loss, humiliation, anxiety, or boredom. Sandro quickly establishes a tie with Claudia rather than allowing himself to mourn the disappearance of Anna. Among the many vicissitudes to which sexuality is exposed, an important one is to divert an interest from an initial object to an interest in a substitute object, which is a simulacrum of the initial object. This is carried out beautifully in the film as Claudia takes on the identity of Anna. She wears her blouse. She dons a brunette wig, and she captures the interest of Anna's lover. Since an unambivalent interest in primary objects cannot be sustained, substitutes become a necessity, but their derivative status implies that they too are unreliable.

Sexuality is also used to bolster the loss of one's self as a striving and integrated person. Sandro destroys the drawing of the young architect, not only out of envious hostility but also in disappointment and in frustration because of his inability to live up to his own ideal self. And it is then that he turns to Claudia for compensatory sex.

Many of the characters cannot sustain interest in any activity for any length of time. The craving for stimulation is followed immediately by attempts to escape, a need for distraction, frivolity, and interest in irrelevancy. Flight and vagabondage are intended to blur anxiety and avoid anguish (Amerio 1964). The emphasis on adventure—as distinguished by the title of the film—highlights the ephemeral quality of the craving. On the most manifest level, the adventure is the trip on the yacht, or perhaps even the search for Anna. At some late point, Sandro, through projection, accuses Claudia of desiring an adventure. It also refers to Sandro's sexual adventure with Gloria Perkins. The notion of an adventure in itself offers a critical commentary on the difficulties of lasting, thorough, and engaged commitment, the opposing and underlying theme.

The deployment of an instrumental sexuality in the film is in keeping with the revision of notions of sexuality in current psychoanalytic discourse. We have moved from a view of sexuality as the primary source of conflict toward a more expansive view. Sexuality has been given a more authentic place as an area within interpersonal relationships. Erotic activity independent of close human ties is recognized as a symptomatic measure of developmental deficiencies in other areas of the personality. Failures in the establishment of object constancy and motives of revenge and sadism highlight the anxiety-alleviating function of sexuality. Secondarily, the psychic intensity falls on the drive rather than the problematic object to which the drive was directed.

In the face of such a relentless critique of erotic love, Claudia's final gesture of forgiveness at the end is to be noted as the only compassionate gesture in the entire film. Claudia appears, albeit hesitatingly, to offer a resigned acceptance to inevitable human frailty.

The method by which Antonioni succeeds, the formal means by which the negative message attains its power, has been the subject of an analysis by Seymour Chatman (1985). He points out that if we were to concern ourselves solely with the theme of Antonioni's work, we would not be struck by its unique character. After all, the films deal with "the difficulty of sustaining a love relationship, of finding work that is meaningful, of weathering the stormy conflict between our own drive and others' expectation of us" (1)—such themes are common in the art of our time. Clearly, it is the manner in which Antonioni expresses these themes that reveals his masterful artistry.

The film begins with a mysterious disappearance and a search for someone who is lost. We wonder: "Where is Anna? What happened to her?" The enigma encourages a search for clues to solve the mystery. However, as the search continues, we soon lose interest in it and begin to find ourselves interested in other things—the landscape, the antique vase, the searchers themselves—these adjunct interests feel irrelevant to the main search. The quest is like a psychoanalytic investigation, the material of which is continually changing. And as the search progresses, we experience varying states of tension. Our anxiety is stimulated and alleviated. We are given partial answers, but experience no sense of resolution.[1] Several times our interest is piqued by the surface phenomena which accompany the narrative, primarily because such surface phenomena are given added intensity by the wish to solve the mystery of the disappearance. The enigmatic quality adds intensity to each sequential visual image as if they are clues leading to the solution. Where there is little narrative continuity established between the sequence of scenes, the emotional impact is increased because of the jarring discontinuity. The minimalization of explanatory dialogue places an extra demand on the viewer to supply a meaningful connecting link. Associations are presented which have an evocative linkage with unconscious content obeying no conscious logical order. The gap in the conscious sequencing is a form through which the emptiness of the personality is deployed.

In one of the early scenes between Anna and Sandro, failure

1. The mechanism of using seemingly trivial hints as a pathway toward understanding—so germane to psychoanalysis—is explored by Ginzburg (1989) in his chapter, "Clues: Roots of an Evidential Paradigm."

of communication is depicted by a bar in his apartment which stands between them. The bar and the early lovemaking are connected by the unsuccessful efforts at overcoming an emotional barrier. In the search for Anna, the emptiness of the island highlights the isolation of the figures; the lack of success in the search for Anna reflects the difficulty in finding fulfillment in the lives of the people. Shortly after Sandro "inadvertently" destroys the drawing by the architectural student, we are presented with a scene of young seminarians being led to a class, a reflection of Sandro's lost opportunity in having sacrificed his earlier ambitions. Through metonymy and displacement, visual elements carry an emotional charge from one scene to another, much as the nocturnal dream uses the mechanisms of the dream work (Metz 1982).

Chatman (1985) quotes Antonioni as stating, "There exists a psychological law which says that to each motion of the soul there corresponds an external motion; to discover these motions is the first task of film authors" (87).[2] Such commentary highlights the importance of the mechanism of condensation as the telling device in producing visual significance as a factor in heightened visual imagery. This is demonstrated in the frontal view of the empty buildings in the scene preceding Sandro and Claudia's lovemaking on the hill. Antonioni stays with this image for a prolonged period of time, and thus provides the mise-en-scène which gives the eroticism its empty, anxious quality even in the midst of exaggerated emotion.

Even more strangely, Antonioni displaces characters from one scene to another. They appear to be moving from left to right in one scene; they are suddenly transposed as if their positions are

---

2. Geoffrey Nowell-Smith also finds an emphasis on delving beneath a surface; "Movements below the surface are generally left to be deduced from surface reactions" (1963–1964, 20).

reversed in the next scene. Mirrors are used for the dislocation of the images. By changing wigs brunettes become blondes, blondes become brunettes, and identities become distorted through this doubling. Similar gestures are repeated, but the meanings are shifted. At the beginning, when Sandro and Anna are making love, she places her hand on the back of his head in a gesture of passion. At the end of the film, Claudia uses a similar gesture to communicate a fainthearted understanding and hesitant forgiveness.

When Antonioni spoke of his work, he spoke like an existentialist. He emphasized the difficulty in forming loving relationships in the spiritually bereft modern world, that modernity, emotional attachment, and full commitment are incompatible. The requirements of contemporary life are incompatible with fulfillment in love or work. This emphasis on meaninglessness in modern life echoes the theme of T. S. Eliot's *The Waste Land*, a literary work which also followed the devastation of a world war, a period during which earlier hopeful expectations for progress were shattered. If we recognize that *L'avventura* appears in a similar historical context, its sense of disillusion becomes more understandable. However, its message is not limited by a historical epoch, and the film's view of the vicissitudes of human relations has a more universal applicability. Psychoanalytically, we note the presence of internalized conflict, the difficulties of establishing a cohesive identity and selfhood. We note the tendency to revert toward regressive pulls toward lack of object constancy and reinstinctualization of archaic forms of sexuality as a means of dealing with anxiety and loss. We note the ubiquity of the need to return to primitive states of undifferentiation and the defensive projection and externalization which legitimize regression and gives it justification. Such views of *L'avventura* do not only emphasize the theme of the collapse of historical values; they also highlight the importance of the psychological anxieties associated with self-definition. Half a century later, we find the message and its transmission has continuing viability. *L'avventura* informs us how prevalent are the means by which the self struggles with dissolution and turns away from the route toward fulfillment.

REFERENCES

Amerio, P. 1964. Antonioni: Appunti per una psicologia dell'irrelevant. In *Michelangelo Antonioni,* ed. Carlo di Carlo. Rome: Edizioni di Bianco e nero. 45–66.

Chatman, S. 1985. *Antonioni, or the Surface of the World.* Berkeley: University of California Press.

Chatman, S. and G. Fink, eds. 1989. *"L'avventura": Michelangelo Antonioni, Director.* New Brunswick, N.J.: Rutgers University Press.

Freud, S. 1912. On the universal tendency to debasement in the sphere of love (Contributions to the psychology of love). *Standard Edition* 11:177–90.

Ginzburg, C. 1989. *Clues, Myths, and the Historical Method.* Baltimore: Johns Hopkins University Press.

Lesser, S. O. 1964. *L'avventura:* A closer look. *Yale Review* 54:41–50.

Metz, C. 1982. *The Imaginary Signifier: Psychoanalysis and the Cinema.* Bloomington: Indiana University Press.

Nowell-Smith, G. 1963–1964. Shape around a black point. *Sight and Sound* 33:16–20.

Samuels, C. T. 1970. An interview with Antonioni. *Film Heritage* 5 (Spring):1–12.

Trosman, H. 1985. *Freud and the Imaginative World.* Hillsdale, N.J.: The Analytic Press.

{ *Seven* }

CITIZEN KANE
AND THE RETURN
of the Lost Object

Although opinion has been divided on whether Citizen Kane *is consid-*ered a masterpiece on the basis of its content or the technical innovations with which it has been credited, its status as a masterpiece has been unquestioned. Filmed by Orson Welles in 1940, when he was only twenty five, it has been ranked as the first of the Ten Best Films in the *Sight and Sound* polls of 1962, 1972, 1982, and 1992. Thus, once having attained its prime status, unlike *L'avventura*, it has never been deposed. It has not responded to changing times or shifts in taste during the past fifty years. Its status is unique.

The extensive literature on the film has concerned itself with a variety of topics. Gregg Toland ([1941] 1991), the film's cinematographer, has offered an extensive description of its techniques, some of which were innovative, some derived from Toland's previous work. Other writers have analyzed at length the relationship between the protagonist and the life of William Randolph Hearst, the publisher whose biography served as a source for many of the incidents in the film (Higham 1970; Kael 1971). The film has been subjected to an analysis in terms of the political events at the time of its making (Mulvey 1992) and varieties of modes of interpretation (Carroll 1989). Still others have speculated about the extent of participation of Welles in the writing of the original script (Kael 1971; Carrington 1978; Rosenbaum 1992)[1] and the film has been viewed from a psychoanalytic perspective as well (Houston 1982; Beja 1985; Mulvey 1992).

A psychoanalytic view of the film must of necessity start with an analysis of the main character, Charles Foster Kane. Welles himself partially disparaged such an approach by referring to the film as "dollar-book Freud," but he added, "nevertheless, it's how I analyze the film"—a partial disclaimer followed by an avowal (Brady 1989, 285). Welles thus was clear about his debt to Freud in the depiction of the character he portrayed. In all likelihood, however, he did not understand that a psychoanalytic approach was more than an understanding of the unconscious of the protagonist. It is the purpose of this chapter to delineate a contemporary analytic view of the main character and to point out the means by which the film succeeds in attaining its powerful aesthetic effect.

The outline of the plot, as in most such instances, gives little understanding of the impact of the film. A prominent and wealthy publisher, Charles Foster Kane, dies at the age of seventy five in his castle on his lavish Florida estate. As he dies, he utters the one word, "Rosebud." A preliminary newsreel is made of his life, but it is unsatisfactory since it is concerned only with the public surface of his biography and lacks an understanding of the man. In order to heighten the impact of the newsreel, a reporter is sent by an editor to find an answer which would

1. Both the shooting script, which was written by Herman J. Mankiewicz and Orson Welles, and the text of the film are published in Pauline Kael's *The Citizen Kane Book* of 1971. In her contribution to the volume, Kael emphasizes that much of the preliminary work on the script was done by Mankiewicz and that he did not get sufficient credit for his contribution. Carrington (1978, 1985) demonstrates that Welles indeed played a highly significant role in changing Mankiewicz's original script and giving it the particular visual impact it achieved.

7.1 Orson Welles's *Citizen Kane*. Courtesy of The Museum of Modern Art/Film Stills Archive.

explain the enigmatic dying word. The reporter interviews Kane's second wife, Susan Alexander, consults the journal of his deceased guardian, Walter Park Thatcher, speaks to a business associate, Mr. Bernstein, who was one of his newspaper editors, an ex-friend, Leland, whom Kane knew since his college days, and Kane's butler, Raymond. None can explain what "Rosebud" means, but the answer is given to the audience at the end of the film. "Rosebud" is the name painted on an old sled which was abandoned at the time his mother sent him off to be raised by Thatcher, and thus refers to what he lost at the age of eight, when he was separated from his mother.

A closer analysis of the film gives us a greater understanding of the means by which the impact of the narrative is heightened. The initial scenes of the film begin with a series of fences accompanied by an excluding "No Trespassing" sign. As the camera penetrates through the barrier of the fences and the "No Trespassing" sign, we get closer and closer to a large castle with a lighted window in the background. Suddenly the light is extinguished, and we then enter a bedroom. The screen is filled with the moving lips of a dying man as he utters the word, "Rosebud." From his hand falls a small rounded glass ornament, a paperweight of a make-believe snow scene and log cabin. As the glass ornament falls, it breaks on the marble floor and we see in the reflected glass a distorted vision of a nurse who enters the room and covers the dead body.

Abruptly we then are introduced to the newsreel, adapted from the format of the late 1930s prototype, "The March of Time." The newsreel, barely disguised as "News on the March," presents film clips of Kane's life. We are told of Kane's fabulous castle, Xanadu, and that his funeral in 1941 was one of the biggest and strangest, and are given a sketch of Kane's life. Snippets of newsreel film present him in a variety of settings. Although fabulously wealthy, he came from humble origins. He was raised by Thatcher, a wealthy banker—"grand old man of Wall Street"—who became his guardian. Kane was a controversial figure; by some he was considered a Communist, by others a Fascist. He saw himself as an American. He was married twice, the first time to the niece of the President of the United States. He was on the brink of an outstanding political career when he was discovered to have had a mistress, whom he kept in a love nest. The scandal ruined his political aspirations. His first wife divorced him, and she and his young son died shortly thereafter in a motor accident. He then married his mistress, whom he coerced into a career as an opera singer. Following a suicide attempt, she also eventually left him. Subsequently during the Depression he lost his newspapers, and he died isolated and friendless at the age of seventy five.

Following the projection room sequence, in pursuit of the meaning of "Rosebud," the barely visible reporter, Thompson, first visits Kane's second wife, Susan, who is now a cabaret singer in a nightclub. Thompson tries to interview Susan, but she is totally unresponsive, and orders him out. A waiter nearby informs Thompson that Susan knows nothing about "Rosebud." Next, Thompson visits the austere and forbidding setting of the memorial library of Kane's guardian, Thatcher, and he is permitted to read through the part of the memoirs describing Thatcher's interactions with Kane. In flashback, the film now visualizes Thatcher's visit in 1871 to the log cabin in Colorado where the young Kane is playing with a sled in the snow. We see Thatcher inside the house with the child's mother and father, and we are informed that a defaulting boarder has left to Mrs. Kane a gold mine, which has become a source of great wealth. The child's mother decides to have the child leave with Thatcher, who will become his legal guardian, and thus she separates the small boy from her and his uneducated and harsh father. When the child threatens Thatcher with his sled, the father says that the boy should be thrashed and the mother states that she is removing the child so that the father cannot get at him. In the next flashback, we are shown that Kane grows to young maturity, decides to run the newspaper *The Enquirer*, and launches an attack on big business, the source of Thatcher's income as well as Kane's. In the Depression, Kane surrenders his newspaper empire to Thatcher, and states that if he had not been born very rich, he really might have become a great man. Thompson, the reporter, finds nothing here to enlighten him about the meaning of "Rosebud." But the stage has been set for imbuing the sled with the capacity for representability in a context of emotional abandonment, resultant hostility, and thwarted ambition.

Next, the reporter visits Bernstein, who is now an old man. Unlike Thatcher, who found Kane an irresponsible irritant, Bernstein idealized him. Bernstein recalls with great pleasure how Kane had taken over *The Enquirer* when it was a stodgy, unsuccessful newspaper, how Bernstein and Leland, Kane's friend, had taken over the newspaper offices and how successful Kane had been in building up circulation by raiding the staff of a rival newspaper, *The Chronicle*, in order to get the best writers. In Bernstein's eyes, Kane was a mixture of a principled man who hoped to help the underprivileged and a charming but unscrupulous populist who early in his career displayed techniques of the yellow journalist to build circulation. As a sign of success, Kane leaves for a trip to Europe, and begins to collect European art, which he ships back. When he returns from Europe, he announces his engagement to the President's niece, Emily Norton, a further valued piece in his collection. When asked, Bernstein states that he does not know to what "Rosebud" refers, but perhaps it has to do with some loss in Kane's life "since he lost almost everything he had." Bernstein directs Thompson to consult Kane's former friend, Leland.

Thompson then visits the hospital where the elderly Leland is receiving nursing care. Leland, in contrast to Bernstein, is unequivocally critical of Kane. He claims Kane behaved like a swine. Through a flashback, we are brought back to the early years of Kane's marriage to Emily. The deterioration of the relationship is presented through memorable short scenes at the breakfast table: we are shown the alienation of the couple by the fact that they move farther and farther apart at the table. Leland also tells us of Kane's meeting with Susan Alexander.

They meet by chance on a street as Kane is about to go to the warehouse where his mother's belongings are stored. He is abruptly muddied by a passing horse and buggy, and Susan invites him to her nearby room and offers to help him clean up. She does not know who he is, but while they sit together, she tells him that her mother wanted her to become a singer. She sings for him, and he amuses her by wiggling his ears and making shadow figures on the wall. He clearly is attracted by her childlike innocence and lack of pretentiousness, and they shortly become lovers. Kane is in the midst of a political campaign for governor of New York. Claiming that his opponent, "Boss" Jim Gettys is corrupt, Kane threatens him with a jail sentence. In retaliation, Gettys threatens to expose Kane's "love nest" unless he withdraws from the gubernatorial campaign. Kane refuses to do so; he believes that the love of the people will be a more decisive factor in his support than his marital infidelity. However, he loses the election, his wife divorces him, and he marries Susan.

Kane next turns his energies to making Susan a great opera star, and insists that she take lessons in spite of her obvious lack of talent. He builds her an opera house in Chicago, but when she performs, she is hopelessly inadequate. By this time, Leland has moved to Chicago, and Leland and Kane have become estranged. When Leland begins to write a negative review of Susan's singing, he falls into a drunken sleep at the typewriter. Kane finishes the negative review, and then fires Leland. Leland tells Thompson that Kane could not love anyone: all his efforts were directed at winning the love of others for himself. But Leland does not know the meaning of "Rosebud" either.

Thompson returns to attempt another interview with Susan in

the nightclub, and now Susan is more cooperative. In another flashback, her singing debut is repeated, and she emphasizes that her opera career was solely Kane's idea. In her despair, she attempts suicide, and Kane finally consents that she need no longer continue her attempt to become an opera star. Kane -builds the palatial Xanadu, but she is bored and lonely, and plays with gigantic jigsaw puzzles. At a picnic, which Kane has proposed to help her with her boredom, shrilly and in anger she points out to him his self-absorbed, narcissistic preoccupations. He slaps her, and she packs and leaves him. In the most affectively moving scene in the film, Kane pleads with her not to leave, but her mind is made up.

The final flashback takes place at Xanadu, and evolves from Thompson's talk with the butler, Raymond. Raymond presents his version of the events following Susan's abandonment of Kane, and we see that Kane in a furious temper tantrum wrecks Susan's room, destroys the furniture, pictures, belongings, and stops only at the point at which he picks up a paperweight and murmurs, "Rosebud." The viewer watching the film for the first time is likely to have great difficulty recognizing that the glass globe is the one which was present in Susan's apartment when Kane and Susan first meet and is the one remnant of his relationship with her which he does not destroy. Kane becomes suddenly quiescent, and walks out of the room past a series of reflecting mirrors in front of his shocked servants. Raymond hopes to make some money out of this revelation, but he does not know the connection between "Rosebud" and the paperweight, so Thompson tells him that the information is not worth much.

Finally, Thompson and a series of reporters and photographers walk through the halls at Xanadu, and note the extensive collection of statues and memorabilia—the massive accumulation of Kane's possessions. They reflect on the failure to find the meaning of "Rosebud," and resignedly Thompson says that perhaps it would not have helped anyway, that a single word cannot explain a man's life. As the reporters leave, the tracking camera picks out the packed crates of Kane's past, photographing the belongings of Kane's mother, and then rests on workmen throwing discarded articles into a furnace. A man throws in the sled, which soon goes up in flames. As the sled burns, with the letters "Rosebud" emblazoned on the surface, we recognize the sled of Kane's childhood. The film ends with a distant view of Xanadu and the sign "No Trespassing," that we saw at the beginning.

THE PSYCHOANALYTIC APPROACH TO THE PERSONALITY OF KANE

Among the attempts to deal with the personality of Kane psychoanalytically, two approaches stand out, that of James Naremore (1978) and that of Laura Mulvey (1992).[2] Mulvey points out that in *Citizen Kane* "themes and symptoms of oedipal conflict and sexual difficulty . . . can only be investigated, deciphered and brought into visibility through psychoanalytic theory" (16). We are presented with a view of an oedipal child who has been separated by his mother at a critical period in his own life and thus has never had an opportunity to experience an oedipal resolution. His erotic interests symbolized by lying prone and sliding on a sled named "Rosebud" are abruptly interrupted.[3] He is forced to leave his

2. Welles often depicted similar characters whose personalities have been well described as "Power Babies" (Houston 1982). Among possible sources of identification of Welles with Kane is the significant fact that both lost their mothers at a similar age.

3. We are informed that "Rosebud" may be partially derived from the knowledge obtained by Welles that William Randolph Hearst had referred to the genitalia of his mistress, Marion Davies, with the term "Rosebud" (Brady 1989, 287).

mother and is exposed to the intervention of an emotionally limited and crassly materialistic father surrogate, Thatcher. The child already had been exposed to paternal sadistic attack at the hands of his putative father, as evidenced by the fact that the latter had threatened to thrash him when he attacks Thatcher.

In fact, a case can be made for James Kane's not being the father in reality. We are informed that the deed to the mine had been left not to both the mother and father but only to Mrs. Kane. Thus we are left with the speculation that there was a special relationship between Fred Graves, the defaulting boarder who stayed with the Kanes, and Mary Kane. Is James Kane in fact the first "foster" father who is threatened by the presence of another man's child in his home? Thus, the separation of the child that takes place in the isolated Colorado setting not only deprives the child of a mother to whom he is attached but also a threatening father surrogate with whom he has already sadistically identified. He has been continuously deprived of a supportive uninterrupted contact with a man who can offer him an opportunity for a positive masculine identification.

Faced with the loss of parenting figures, the growing child and young man continues to deny the loss and tries to reestablish substitutes for what is experienced as a lack. His interest in a newspaper with a mass circulation is an attempt to control a large readership which will compensate him for the love of a parent. In addition, he fills the emptiness in his life by amassing an infinite number of possessions. He continuously resents the presence of Thatcher, the surrogate father figure, whose foster child he also becomes. When he takes over the newspaper, he disposes of the editor, whom he sees as ineffectual as the earlier father who could not protect him. In order to increase his circulation and influence, he usurps from his rival newspaper the men who had made it strong.

Although sexuality is hinted at only symbolically by displacement in the early childhood scene, it was more apparent in the original version of the *Citizen Kane* script, before it was censored. The party celebrating the triumph over the rival newspaper takes place in a brothel scene; it was subsequently transformed into a dinner with chorus girls in the place of prostitutes.

When Kane meets Susan as his marriage to Emily is threatened because of her intolerance for his attack on her uncle, the President, Kane is on his way to the warehouse to examine the belongings of his mother, which have been stored there. Clearly Susan is an erotic object who replaces his mother, but in fact she also activates the longings of the young Kane who strives to succeed, particularly when she speaks of her mother as having had ambitions for her to become a singer. When his political ambitions come to naught, he forms an identification with the ambitious maternal figure, and thus he brings her back to life. He seizes the opportunity to help the innocent young girl become the singer her mother wanted her to become. Just as he wanted to become an outstanding publisher and help the poor and undertrodden through his crusade against injustice, he will now devote himself to the task of bringing out the latent talent in Susan. Throughout his life, he rails against the fathers who interfere with maternal attachments and identifications: Thatcher who takes him from his mother, Gettys the politician who is his rival for the love of the people, Leland the critic who finds Susan's singing wanting, Susan's singing teacher who tries to point out the reality of Susan's limitation, and finally Susan herself who is abused by his ambitious preoccupations for her.

A reading in terms of an attachment to his mother, with resultant identification with her is clear throughout the film and is readily apparent to the psychoanalytic reader. His fixation is marked by the appearance of the paperweight ornament at the beginning of the film as Kane dies, at the point at which Susan first enters Kane's life, and its reemergence after he destroys her room when she abandons him. The attempt at repression of the conflict has its visual representation as well, and is revealed in the presence of snow used as a form of concealment of the conflict, keeping it buried in a nascent state.

We are presented with other components of Kane's personality which is susceptible to regressive retreat and imprinted with pregenital and narcissistic components. His anal retentive interests find expression in compulsive acquisition of objects (Naremore 1978). Kane cannot tolerate a relationship which is based on mutuality. He finds his first wife while embarked on a European tour dedicated to a vast purchase of works of art, which then become stored. She too is an impersonal object to him. His unmodulated sadism is expressed in the violent temper tantrum when Susan leaves; he is like a raging child destroying what deprives him of an organized self, the necessary partially externalized other (Kohut 1972).

Kane compensates for his vulnerability and brittleness by narcissistic grandiosity. He sees himself as a potential leader of men, a crusader who will liberate those unfortunates whom he must protect and who need his support. When Gettys threatens him with exposure and the likelihood that he will lose his family and the election, Kane believes the threat is an idle one because he is "Charles Foster Kane," the people will rally around him, and he will have unlimited support. When they do not, he turns his back on the people and feels the dismal disappointment of the frustrated and abandoned child. When it is clear that Susan has no talent for singing, he cannot face the reality of her limited talent but insists that "she must show them" so that he will not be humiliated following her failure. He then retreats to a fantasy castle, claiming self-sufficiency and consolation in lonely seclusion. Thus "Rosebud" is not only a sexual symbol, but also a sign of the stunted and arrested self that never comes to full bloom.

A PSYCHOANALYTIC APPROACH TO THE FORM OF THE FILM

To emphasize the personality of Kane is to subscribe to one facet of a psychoanalytic approach. The psychoanalytic instrument can also be used to examine the structure and the form of the film. The outward frame of the story, the search for the meaning of "Rosebud" and the attempt to understand Kane are the tasks which give structure to the film. The investigative reporter Thompson is sent by his editor Ralston, to penetrate the mystery and to make a discovery. Thus, it is no accident that the film begins with a fence that bars access and a sign stating "No Trespassing." The spectator, through the lens of the camera, must disregard the fence, pass through it, and transgress into the "No Trespassing" area. When Thompson first intrudes on the privacy of Susan in her half-drunken and ambivalent grief, the camera, accompanied by a flash of lightning, penetrates into the night-club through the skylight of the room in which she sits. The metaphor of "penetrating the mystery" is presented visually through the technique of the dissolve shot.

Similarly, the deep-focus cinematography provides a range for depth of action which relates past to present. Psychological distance is given a concrete spatial dimension. Among the extensive technical innovations and stylistic devices of the film, particular emphasis has been attached to the utilization of deep focus cinematography. There are many examples of it, and it is particularly noted in the scene in which Kane's mother abandons him to the care of Thatcher. The scene opens with a view of the boy playing joyfully with his sled in the snow, and then as the camera moves forward into our space, we see that we are looking through a window; we see Kane's mother, Thatcher, and the father as they sign the papers legalizing his abandonment. While the action takes place in the foreground, we continue to see the presence of the child through the window in the background, as ironically he sings "The Union Forever." The deep-focus photography illuminates simultaneously the iron will of the mother who works very hard to supress her emotion, the innocence of the boy who does not know what is happening to him, and the dissolution of the family unity which is about to take place. The snow itself communicates the emotional coldness and gloomy colorlessness of the act. The depth of field is the means for establishing connections of disparate components of a scene, an example of a linkage of cumulative emotional currents—the joyful play and the ominous threat coldly observed—critical events in the narrative.

In addition to deep-focus, camera shots were done from low levels to heighten the verticality of figures, rooms were given a heightened sense of claustrophobic reality, and ceilings were included in the mise-en-scène. In fact, some of the shots were done by a camera from below floor level to increase the sense of views as perceived by a small child. Welles found the contribution of his cinematographer, Gregg Toland, so innovative and daring that Welles gave Toland a special billing at the end of the credits for the photography, an unusual gesture for a producer-director to offer a cinematographer.

The ordering of the events of the flashbacks makes a dramatic impact which can best be described in terms of a regressive reconstruction. On the surface, the flashbacks seem to follow a chronological order, beginning with the latency-aged child as he is depicted in Thatcher's memoirs and ending with Kane as an old man when he is abandoned by Susan. We first meet Kane as a young man at his zenith in the triumph as a newspaper publisher who overcomes his masculine rivals, who stand in his way and whom he wishes to usurp. His heterosexual and oedipal triumphs, however, soon become hollow victories. In his death, he reestablishes the early maternal connection, which is the deepest part of his personality.

The regressive return is not only presented to us as a clarification of Kane's personality, but is the result of the search itself. Where Thompson fails in his effort to become enlightened, the members of the audience succeed. We, the viewers, take on the role of the successful investigator, enlightened by the emblem on the burning sled. Establishing a referent for the signifier "Rosebud" allows us to form a hypothetical reconstruction, but this reconstruction is to be further evaluated.

In concert with this hypothetical interpretation and in view of Thompson's final statement of doubt regarding the truth value of dying words, the empirical viewer is left to puzzle about the adequacy of the interpretation. Indeed how much is explained by the burning sled? Can such a method of investigation lead to valid results?[4] The viewer in the audience identifies with the barely visible Thompson, our surrogate, who wants to discover a solution. But he keeps a skeptical mind. The film resembles *L'avventura* (See chapter 6) in that both films are concerned with a search and it is the search that organizes the narrative structure. In *L'avventura*, the search is given up. Almost as an expression of its hopelessness and emptiness, diversion soon sets in and the

4. N. Carroll (1989) leaves room for what he refers to as the Rosebud interpretation and "the enigma interpretation." The Rosebud interpretation claims we can understand Kane. The enigma interpretation cautions skepticism. Carroll wants to leave open a view of the film as an attempt "to animate a debate. Specifically, it is designed rhetorically to draw the audience into consideration of the conflicting claims of two commonplace views about human life" (57). This is a view of the film as facilitating a dialogue and providing a choice for the spectator. Unfortunately, Carroll moves from this interesting view to the notion that the film is a response to Clement Greenberg's paper "Avant-Garde and Kitsch" of 1939, refuting the notion that high art could not simultaneously be popular (Greenberg [1939] 1961).

searchers become enmeshed in their own substituted concerns. Thompson in *Citizen Kane* is relentless, continues the search, and resists the temptation that Susan offers him at the end of telling her about his life. He is interested in decipherment, and although skeptical and frustrated in his curiosity, he maintains an inquisitive analytic stance. Like the psychoanalyst, he maintains a condition of neutrality, but exercises subjective judgment. Like the analyst, he is a skeptic who is looking for understanding of something that remains a mystery.

Thompson and the camera in *Citizen Kane* become a means for probing the blend of fantasy and reality. The fantasy of the castle and the reality of the newsreel are similar to the blend that one finds in the personality of Kane himself. To this extent, the film is a reflection of that particular narcissistic preoccupation when external object interest and subjectivity have become an amalgam. Rosebud and the glass ball are the mixture of the lost reality of childhood and the adult fantasy which represents and retains it.

In summary, many believe that Orson Welles's *Citizen Kane* is an outstanding masterpiece if not "the best film ever made." Its status can be partially explained by the clarity with which a psychoanalytic approach can be applied to the protagonist. In addition, the technique of the film allows the spectator to participate in a psychoanalytic investigation and to question the significance of its endeavors. The film empowers the spectator with a degree of knowledge superior to that of the participants in the narrative. The technical skill with which it presents its story offers a sense of enlightenment in a context of skepticism.

The mistress of William Randolph Hearst, the publisher upon whose life many of the events of the film are based, wrote an autobiography. Marion Davies, who to some extent shared some of Hearst's antipathy to the film because of its similarity to their lives, stated, "I never saw the picture *Citizen Kane*, but my sister

Rose did, and she said, 'I'll kill him [referring to Orson Welles]; it's terrible. You can't even see the picture because it's all dark.' " Orson Welles, thirty-five years after completing *Citizen Kane*, wrote a foreword to Marion Davies's autobiography, *The Times We Had: Life with William Randolph Hearst* (1975), and referred to her in affectionate and glowing terms, as a "princess . . . an accomplished comedienne . . . a delightful person," and he was at pains to point out her dissimilarity to Susan Kane. It is no wonder that he could be magnanimous. By means of an imaginative elaboration of a piece of mundane reality—the reality of their lives—he had been able to create his masterpiece.

REFERENCES

Beja, M. 1985. Where you can't get at him: Orson Welles and the attempt to escape from father. *Literature/Film Quarterly* 13:1:2–9.

Brady, F. 1989. *Citizen Welles: A Biography of Orson Welles*. New York: Charles Scribner's Sons.

Carrington, R. 1978. The scripts of *Citizen Kane*. *Critical Inquiry* 5:369–400.

———. 1985. *The Making of Citizen Kane*. Berkeley: University of California Press.

Carroll, N. 1989. Interpreting *Citizen Kane*. *Persistence of Vision* 7:51–62.

Davies, M. 1975. *The Times We Had: Life with William Randolph Hearst*. Foreword by Orson Welles. Indianapolis/New York: Bobs Merrill.

Greenberg, C. [1939] 1961. *Avant-Garde and Kitsch in Art and Culture*. Boston: Beacon Press.

Higham, C. 1970. *The Film of Orson Welles*. Berkeley: University of California Press.

Houston, B. 1982. Power and dis-integration in the films of Orson Welles. *Film Quarterly* 35:2–12.

Kael, P. 1971. *The Citizen Kane Book*. New York: Limelight Editions.

Kohut, H. 1972. Thoughts on narcissism and narcissistic rage. *The Psychoanalytic Study of the Child* 27:360–400.

Mulvey, L. 1992. *Citizen Kane*. London: British Film Institute.

Naremore, J. 1978. *The Magic World of Orson Welles.* New York: Oxford University Press.

Rosenbaum, J. 1992. *This Is Orson Welles: Orson Welles and Peter Bogdanovich.* New York: Harper Collins.

Toland, G. [1941] 1991. Realism for *Citizen Kane. American Cinematographer* (August): 37–42. Originally published in February 1941.

8.1 Alfred Hitchcock's *Vertigo*. Courtesy of The Museum of Modern Art/Film Stills Archive.

{ *Eight* }

VERTIGO AND

the Enabling Fantasy

Alfred Hitchcock was fond of a screen memory he often reported. He said that at five he had committed an act deserving reprimand. For punishment, his father sent him to the local police station with a note to the chief of police, who then obligingly locked the little boy in a cell, for about five or ten minutes. He was told, "This is what we do with naughty boys" (Spoto 1983, 9; Truffaut 1983, 25). Hitchcock presented the story as an example of a cruel father having scarred a child for life. It was told often enough and with such apparent satisfaction as to convince others that "it probably never happened" (Spoto 1983, 374). Whether blandly mythologizing or relentlessly castigating, the tale fixes a theme which resonates throughout his work. Whatever the reality of the abuse, the screen memory has the earmark of a typical Hitchcock plot. The protagonist is duped into playing the role of a victim, largely as a result of his own doing. At some point, however, the deception is exposed, and the seeming reality turns out to be an illusion, an artifice meant to be eventually deciphered and exposed. Quite clearly, in Hitchcock's own case, rather than being "scarred for life," the childhood drama—whether fantasy or real—becomes a central theme for his films. Fantasy itself becomes the subject of his work. Nowhere is this more in evidence than in the film which is generally accepted to be his masterpiece, *Vertigo*.

Vertigo, which was made in 1957 and released in 1958, is generally accepted to be the supreme example of Hitchcock's work after he came to America, an excellent example of the complex interaction between the real, the fantastic, and the blurring of the distinction between the two.

A contemporary psychoanalytic perspective takes into account the developmental steps by which a sense of reality becomes a constituent of the mature ego, and finds a film like *Vertigo* highly pertinent to its current preoccupations. It is apparent that reality testing develops in response to the need to replace lost objects of satisfaction with substitutes. A sense of external reality cannot be considered as a faculty of the mind that is independent of need, desire, and internal structures that constitute psychic reality. In a word, reality is constructed, and it is constructed with the forms imposed by the experiences and memories of early gratifications and their frustration. *Vertigo* demonstrates how the compelling search for the lost object finds its place in the composition of a sense of reality.

Although the original story of *Vertigo* is based on a novel, *D'Entre les Mortes*, by Pierre Boileau and Thomas Narcejac, it was revised for the screenplay by Alec Coppel and even more extensively by Samuel Taylor, who wrote the version upon which Hitchcock based his film. Taylor, however, pointed out that it was largely the work of Hitchcock (1991).[1] The critical narrative decisions were made by him, and thus it is to be conceived as largely the product of his own creativity.

---

1. Taylor saw the film for the first time since 1958, and participated in a three-day conference on the rereleased films of Hitchcock in 1986. It was on that occasion that he credited Hitchcock with major participation in the script. His comment, "*Vertigo* is the most horrible practical joke ever played on a man" (1991, 288), suggests a connection with Hitchcock's screen memory.

The film opens with a chase across the rooftops of some tall buildings in San Francisco. Two policemen, one in uniform, the other a detective in a business suit, Scottie Ferguson, are chasing a fleeing criminal. As Scottie leaps from one building to another, he trips, and hangs precariously from a gutter far above a distant street level. He is too frightened to give a hand to the policeman who offers to help him up. The policeman slips and falls to the ground, and is presumably killed.

In the next scene, Scottie is with his friend Midge, a commercial artist to whom he was once engaged and who still loves him. He has somehow been rescued from his precarious perch, and is recovering from his injuries. But he has been left with a severe acrophobia, and has now resigned from the police department. He tells Midge that an old college friend, Gavin Elster, has asked him to call. Scottie does so, and finds that Gavin is now in the shipbuilding business but concerned about his wife Madeleine, who is acting strangely. She believes that she is possessed by a spirit from the past, her great-grandmother Carlotta. Elster asks Scottie to follow her and discern her movements. Although Scottie is reluctant to do so, he complies with Elster's request.

As he tracks her through the streets of San Francisco, she goes to a flower shop where she buys a corsage, to a cemetery where she stands in front of the grave of Carlotta, to the art museum at the Palace of the Legion of Honor where she sits in front of Carlotta's portrait, and to an old hotel where he loses her. In the art museum, Scottie notices the identical nature of Madeleine's corsage and hairdo swirl to the corsage and the swirl of hair of Carlotta in the portrait. Scottie finds from an authority on San Francisco history that Carlotta had been abandoned in the middle of the last century by a wealthy man who had taken her child from her, and then had suicided.

The next time Scottie follows Madeleine, she drives to the foot of the Golden Gate Bridge and throws herself into the water. He rescues her and carries her back to his apartment, where he undresses her and puts her to bed. When she awakes, he tells her who he is. When he leaves to answer the phone in another room, she flees, but returns the next day to thank him for the rescue. He is more and more attracted to her, is puzzled by her strange behavior as they continue to meet, and soon falls in love with her. She tells him of a frightening dream of walking down a mirrored corridor toward an open grave which waits for her in a scene with a bell tower.

Midge, Scottie's friend, becomes jealous of his interest in Madeleine. On his next visit to Midge's apartment, she displays a portrait that she has painted of her own face superimposed on the body of Carlotta. Scottie reacts very negatively to this travesty; he sees it as a parodic derision of his feelings toward someone he has begun to revere.

Madeleine appears at Scottie's apartment during the night, and tells him she had the dream about the bell tower again, this time identifying it sufficiently for Scottie to be able to recognize it as a real place, the mission San Juan Bautista, about one hundred miles south of San Francisco. In his interest to help her dispel the feeling of being possessed, he urges her to accompany him to the mission. When they arrive, Scottie shows her that the elements of her dream are based on the reality of the scene. But when he expresses his love for her, she runs off toward the top of the tower. As he climbs the stairs after her, because of his acrophobia, he cannot reach the top. He hears a scream, and watches a body fall far below. He leaves the scene in horror as the body is discovered.

The next scene depicts a coroner's hearing which renders a verdict of suicide. The coroner blames Scottie for his weakness in having been unable to rescue Madeleine from her suicide. Scottie is mortified and guilt-ridden, and subsequently has nightmares which resemble Madeleine's dreams. He dreams of the cemetery, the open grave, and is tormented by a vision of the fall from the roof. He spends a year under psychiatric care, and is unresponsive to Midge's attempts to help him by her maternal solicitations.

After Scottie is released from the hospital, he continues to be preoccupied with Madeleine. He follows women on the street who remind him of her, and when he finds a woman who, although now dark-haired and dressed differently, resembles Madeleine, he follows her to her hotel room. Initially she rejects his overtures, she tells him her name is Judy Barton, but he persists. She agrees to go out with him. After he leaves her hotel room, Judy decides to flee, and she writes a letter to Scottie revealing the plot in which he was a pawn. Judy is actually Madeleine; she had been coached to play the role of Elster's wife, and Elster had devised a scheme of murdering his wife on top of the tower and throwing her down to her death. Elster knew that Scottie was acrophobic, and that he would experience panic as he was following Judy up the staircase. Thus, he would be unaware that Judy had not been killed. After Judy explains the plot in the letter, she decides to tear it up, hoping that she can win Scottie back because of her love for him.

As Scottie and Judy begin a relationship, he is obsessed with wanting to turn her into an exact replica of Madeleine. At first she resists, but he persists. He buys her flowers and clothes, and he insists that she wear the same gray suit that Madeleine had worn. She, however, wants to be loved for herself. Scottie is fixed on his need to recreate Madeleine, and finally focuses on her hair, insisting that she be blonde rather than brunette and that the hair be shaped in the same manner. She finally relents, believing that in giving up her own identity—"I don't care about me," she says—she will win his total love. When she finally prepares her hair in the same fashion, with the same spiral-like back knot worn by Madeleine, he kisses her passionately and reexperiences the fulfillment he felt when he had kissed Madeleine at San Juan Bautista.

Shortly thereafter, as Scottie watches Judy dress for dinner, he is astonished to note that she is about to don the same necklace which appeared in the portrait of Carlotta in the museum. Now he is fully conscious of the fact that he has been duped, that Judy is actually the woman who played the part of Madeleine. He insists that they go back to the mission, telling Judy that it is necessary for him to return in order for him to be free. When they arrive, he forces her up the tower. And although there is a temporary return of his symptom of panic, he manages to surmount his anxiety, and they arrive at the top, where he confronts her with the plot. In a bitter rage, he tells Judy that he understands now that she had been Elster's mistress, that she had been made to play the part of Madeleine, and that he had been used as a foil in the murder plot. Judy pleads with him that she loves him and wants to forget the past. But as he kisses her, Judy—frightened by a noise of someone who emerges from the dark—falls backwards to her death. As a nun enters, she tolls the death knell, and Scottie stands on the edge of the tower and looks down the great height, free of his phobia.

THE PERSONALITY OF SCOTTIE

The power of unconscious fantasy in *Vertigo* is such as to dissuade an audience from considering issues of plausibility of plot. The imaginative propensity of an audience willing to engage in suspension of disbelief can easily cause us to overlook the unlikelihood of the depicted events. In fact, we share with Scottie an initial skepticism as he accepts Elster's assignment. However, we are soon manipulated and encouraged to displace our disbelief from the conception that Carlotta is a ghost who has come back to haunt Madeleine to a belief in an imposter who can successfully manipulate Scottie. How could he have fallen for such an improbable deception?

Quite clearly, Scottie is unbalanced, literally and psychologically. He is a man of almost fifty, hardly able to keep up with the criminal whom he is inappropriately chasing over the rooftops. Although he apparently had been engaged to Midge when they were in college together many years ago, he is still unattached although he claims he is still "available." His acrophobia has interfered with his capacity to work and he becomes a man in search of a cure. While he is at Midge's apartment, he believes that he can overcome his vertigo by standing on a small ladder and reexperiencing the sensation of looking down from a height, initially, a slight height; however, when Midge inappropriately increases the height for him, the anxiety becomes overwhelming and he falters. Simple behavioral approaches are inadequate. Presented with Elster's request, he is intrigued by the challenge of helping a woman who is also ill and is possessed by the past. His own past, of which we know nothing except that in an indirect way he is responsible for the death of the policeman who tried to rescue him, still haunts him. His attraction to the case of a person haunted by someone dead activates the wish to cure himself through curing Madeleine. He, like her, sees himself as a wanderer. As Madeleine wanders, she cannot break free of the object which has her in thrall, and she finds herself engaged in behavior which duplicates that of the lost Carlotta. Scottie, in following her, duplicates her activity. When he rescues her after her fall into the bay, he repeats her action and turns the fear of falling into a volitional dive. When he believes that Madeleine dies, he repeats her dream, and he returns to the sites that she had visited.

It is not difficult to view Scottie's interest in Madeleine as a special type of choice of object made by men (S. Freud 1910). Scottie has not been able to commit himself to the maternal figure of Midge, who is practical and down-to-earth, but he becomes passionately interested in the mysterious Madeleine, who is the sick wife of another man in need of rescue. His love is based on similarity of need. She serves as a means for his own cure and thus becomes the route through which he establishes his relationship with her.

His conception of cure is based on the notion that Madeleine's tie to the past has to be broken by pointing out that her fantasy is based on real experience. The yoke that she imagines herself to be bound by can only be broken by replacing her fantasy and dreams by their origins in reality. His conception is similar to the current notion of the behavioral treatment of post-traumatic stress disorder. By providing Madeleine with a direct tie to present reality, he believes that he can break the hold that binds her to the past.

After Scottie is censured for Madeleine's death by the coroner, in fact, he has a dream which reveals that unconsciously he has knowledge that he has been duped. Madeleine does not appear in the dream this time. Elster and Carlotta regard him in a hostile manner. Scottie had been caught up in the plot and becomes a foil because of his great need to cure himself. He resists his unconscious knowledge, however, until the point when he can no longer do so. Because his reality testing is still intact, when Judy dons the necklace which gives her away, the need to maintain the tie to the surrogate image is given up.

Toward the latter third of the film, Scottie has sufficiently overcome his guilt concerning the death of his would-be rescuer to be able to assume the role of a figure who is himself in control. He becomes like Elster, a master who transforms a woman. Feminist criticism has been clear in pointing out how Scottie's treatment of Madeleine is clearly an exploitation fraught with misogynistic implications and rationalized by Scottie's repeated insistence that Madeleine comply to alleviate his despair—"do it for me, it can't mean that much to you" (Trumpener 1991).[2]

To what are we to ascribe the cure of Scottie's phobia? At the

2. Hitchcock—no slouch at promoting the controlling active in the face of the passive—corrected the remark attributed to him at one point, denying that he said that "actors are cattle." He stated, "It's a confounded lie. All I said was that they should be *treated* like cattle" (Tomlinson 1991, 107).

point at which he forces Judy to ascend to the tower, he is so preoccupied with accusations directed toward her and the need to replicate and correct the previous ascent with Madeleine, it appears that his rage carries him forward. In fact, it is with a sense of surprise that he notes his full ascent. He has changed from a passive position to one in which he is now the active participant. The difference rests on the fact that he too success-fully has created a surrogate, an amalgam composed of the Madeleine that was and the Judy who is. In fact, he addresses her in a parapraxis as "Maddy," an excellent example of the compromise formation he has effected. He has not given in to the delusional belief that Madeleine has been fully recreated, nor can he accept Judy, the accomplice to a murder, who now offers him love. Since he has no further need for his creation or the material out of which she was formed, it is no wonder that he is not able to restrain Judy when she falls to her death.

THE ROLE OF THE ENABLING FANTASY

The attraction which *Vertigo* holds for psychoanalysis—particu-larly even more in its current form—is due to the importance we attribute to the central position of fantasy in the construction of reality and the role of fantasy in artistic creativity.

The term fantasy is used to denote a quality of the imagination as well as a form in which drives and their fulfillment can be represented either in daydreams or unconsciously (Laplanche and Pontalis 1973). Clearly, in *Vertigo* we see both aspects of the term used. Scottie objects to Midge, a commercial artist who denies her imagination and makes ads for brassieres. He chas-tises her because she has neglected her painting. The practical Midge is presented as a contrast to the mysterious Madeleine, who is guided by fantastic elements which deny reality. Is Made-leine really possessed? Does she disappear when she enters the hotel and Scottie cannot find her? Is she an incarnation of Carlotta, of whom she has no consciousness? Does her allure depend on a recreation of a repressed connection discernable in a double (S. Freud 1919)?

On first viewing the film, when we initially see Judy Barton, we do not accept that she is Madeleine, especially since we believe Madeleine is dead. In fact, Judy's appearance is so altered in hair color and style, expression, clothes, and voice pattern, that we believe Scottie, out of his great need to establish a simulacrum for Madeleine, has found a different person.[3] When we soon discover our error—in the next scene when Judy writes the unmailed letter to Scottie—our attention is subsequently directed to recreating the earlier false identity.

It is striking how far the film takes us in the direction of conceiving a fantasy as the route toward cure. The several sequences involved in Scottie's pursuit of Madeleine heighten the conception of her as unreal, a figure imbued with qualities from the past, as if from another world. The purchase of the bouquet, the trip to the cemetery, the preoccupation with the portrait in the museum, the sudden jump into the bay, the walk in the forest, the trip to the mission, and her enigmatic statements about death all are presented in the context which simultaneously contrasts her with the prosaic reality of the figure of Midge. In hindsight, we are not quite sure whether Madeleine runs from Scottie to ascend the tower in order to fulfill the task set for her by Elster or to interrupt his plan to murder his wife.

---

3. Hitchcock had wanted Vera Miles for the female lead in *Vertigo* but settled for Kim Novak when Miles became pregnant. Although Novak was not a strong actress, Hitchcock exploited her uncertainty. A more skilled actress would have been able to project a more decisive transformation and thus decrease the ambiguity. Taylor (1991) stated, "After all I knew the 'non-acting' qualities of Kim Novak when I started because I had done a picture with her before. So I knew what I was up against. . . . Actually, I think Kim Novak was awfully right" (291–92).

In any case, we can only consider this issue in retrospect. At the time she acts, she appears to be motivated by other-worldly impulses.

The last third of the film is an attempt to change the reality back into the fantasy. Judy, who concretizes her reality by displaying her Kansas driving license, is subsequently transformed to approximate more and more the unreal Madeleine and even the distant Carlotta. In fact, the act of donning the necklace is simultaneously an adoption of the identity of Carlotta, who wears the necklace in the portrait.[4] At the moment when Judy dons the necklace and asks Scottie to fasten it for her she has once again become Madeleine possessed by Carlotta. Thus, the film constantly plays with the theme of stretching the imagination to its utmost and yet keeping it within the realm of the real. The visual dimension of film, with its capacity to visualize and replicate concrete objects, prevents the fantastic from becoming immaterial and thus nonveridical.[5]

It has been pointed out that almost throughout the entire film the audience sees through the eyes of Scottie (Mulvey 1989). Thus, from overcoming our original skepticism that Madeleine is possessed, we are gradually led to the point of accepting the importance of dispelling the fantasy which has been implanted in Madeleine's mind. The emphasis becomes one of alleviating

4. We are never quite sure how the necklace in a portrait which apparently hangs in the museum ever got to Judy. We are never shown the necklace worn by Madeleine. Are we to assume that Elster copied the necklace for Madeleine? And how did the portrait ever manage to get into the museum if it was part of Elster's plot to begin with? Plausibility is beside the point.

5. It is in contrast to the materiality of the film that the titles at the beginning present us with visual images which are nonveridical. As the titles splash on the screen, we see lips, an eye, and then an abstract spiraling figure which enters the eye and which is repeated subsequently in the film in the knot of Madeleine's and Judy's hair. Quite clearly, the spiraling is a reference to the vertigo, the fear of falling, the abyss at the bottom. Although the lips are shut tight, the eye becomes the organ through which penetration takes place.

distress. Somehow, as Madeleine frees herself, Scottie too will free himself. The most noticeable shift in the preoccupation with Scottie's viewpoint occurs at the point at which Judy writes the letter revealing that she was an accomplice in the murder. The emphasis then shifts to one in which we become preoccupied with what Scottie will experience and what he will do when he finds out. Will he be satisfied with the surrogate Madeleine that he has created or will he opt for a confrontation with the woman who has duped him? Will he be freed or further enthralled? Once Scottie has created his Madeleine what role will the ensuing sexual fulfillment play? Scottie has a need to fully relive and reexperience the relationship with Madeleine after he meets Judy. When Scottie turns Judy into Madeleine, it is not sufficient for him simply to repeat some aspects of the past experience with Madeleine or simply recall the experience through the promotion and the recovery of memories and in this way to reconstruct the past in his mind.

The issue of reliving, repeating, and reexperiencing in the form of memory traces cuts to the core of much current psychoanalytic thinking. How much of the psychoanalytic situation is a reenactment of a similar situation from the past in the form of actual behavior and experience? How much is a recollection in the form of memory traces and parts of the experience in the form of isolated images? In the development of psychoanalytic technique, this was a major concern which led to the estrangement between Sigmund Freud and Sandor Ferenczi. Freud believed that too much emphasis on enactments might actually interfere with the efficacy of the psychoanalytic situation (Hoffer 1991). The film is quite clear in stating that Scottie must enact, and the inference is that situations of realistic trauma require such reenactments. It is of interest how cinematographic technique makes use of visualization as a means for representing remembering. When Scottie sees the necklace, we are presented with a visualization of the portrait of Carlotta. When Scottie kisses Judy after she has fully assumed the appearance of Madeleine, Hitch-cock records the scene in a 360-degree view, where the camera and we as viewers totally circle the lovers as they embrace. Simultaneously, we see a depiction of the livery stable at San Juan Bautista, where Scottie had previously kissed Madeleine before she ascends to the tower. Both sequences impart the idea that Scottie experiences memory traces, remembering something that happened previously. We are left to consider that he visual-izes an illusory reality as we do when we see the scenes projected on the screen. Such scenes, brilliantly carried out in *Vertigo*, can be justified by the fact that Scottie must use drastic means in order to cure himself of his obsession. Remembering alone is not sufficient; reliving, reenactment, and repeating are necessary companions.

Hitchcock commented on Judy's reluctance to comply with Scottie's wish to have her *completely* agree to adopt the physical appearance of Madeleine. Judy objects all along to being trans-formed back into Madeleine, as she previously had been by Elster, and her final resistance is only overcome when she con-sents to do her hair with the same spiraling knot she had worn as Madeleine. Hitchcock told François Truffaut that her holding back meant "she still won't take her knickers off" (Truffaut 1983, 244); that is, she will not appear as totally naked as she was when he undressed her after she had been rescued. In a word, Scottie wanted her to submit to him totally so that he could make love to her, and when she complies, he feels himself to be back where he was with Madeleine. When she finally complies, she appears to him as a fantasy figure whom he sees through a hazy light. It is evident that once he takes possession of her body, he needs her to play this role no longer.

As stated earlier, the presence of Scottie's dream after the inquest implies that unconsciously he understood he had been duped all along. The revelation of a murder concealed as a suicide could not take place until the full enactment of the transformation of Judy had occurred. And in the absence of cues, the visual perceptual system could not be brought into play. In a word, the fantasy must be allowed to have free rein, uncontaminated by perceptual fact until a working-through process has occurred within the psyche. There is a striking similarity to the clinical psychoanalytic process. Just as the analysand engages in a transference commitment, which is made up partly of remnants from the past attached to contemporaneous attribute of the analytic situation and the analyst, Scottie goes through an intense experience with a surrogate who is built upon the attributes of a real person. Although the transference imago is based on residues from the past, it must make use of the reality of the figure of the analyst. Such reality includes an essential component of subjectivity, often in the form of enactments which provide a source for projection.

From the psychoanalytic perspective, *Vertigo* offers us comments on the distinction and blending between psychic reality, fantasy, and perceptual material reality. Freud (1915) warned us not "to equate perceptions by means of consciousness with the unconscious mental processes which are their object. Like the physical, the psychical is not necessarily in reality what it appears to us to be" (171). The readiness with which Scottie is prone to accept the material reality of Madeleine, and the need to duplicate her through the transformation of Judy, is an indication of Scottie's need to project his psychic reality upon the external world. Psychic reality is not opposed to material reality; it heightens its intensity. Should the external reality—as in the case of Madeleine—already be a misrepresentation, the misrepresentation can be used as a convenient prop for projection. In a sense, Hitchcock offers multiple views by which psychic reality can be understood. He told his biographer, Spoto (1983), "I really made the film in order to get through to this subtle quality of a man's dreamlike nature" (399), and several times in the film he reminds us that the film itself is a fantasy, as when Madeleine disappears in the hotel, as when he deconstructs our sense of imaginative visual reality by appearing as himself, as when he introduces camera angles such as a zoom-in, track-out shot of the stairwell or a 360-degree circular view of the kiss. At other times, however, he suggests that psychic reality is the lens through which we view external material reality. The telling image here is the repetition in the last part of the film of the events which duplicate, through his transformation of Judy, the earlier encounter with Madeleine. This repetition is an illustration of the ubiquity of the phenomenon of transference, the fact that present-day perceptions are based on anlage which are already present in the mind and which are imposed upon external reality. The discreet and separate contents of the mind, such as internal object representations, give shape to the reality in which we live. *Vertigo* explores the fantasies such embodiments create and the need to test reality continuously in order to determine whether the fantasy is modifiable, correctable, changeable, and compatible with the reality principle.

Unconscious fantasy, the central component of psychic reality, is critical in the creation of the work of art (Segal 1991). Much of artistic creativity depends on the exploitation of the content of unconscious fantasy and the capacity to transform such raw material into imaginative constructions. Fantasies present in the form of images and memories, dreams and daydreams, become imaginative elaborations which lead to new forms, characteristic of art.

The presence of fantasy as a factor in creativity is suggested in Hitchcock's screen memory. Hitchcock frequently played with the ironic intertwining of fantasy and reality. The introduction of himself as a real person in a cameo appearance slightly interrupts the story and heightens the awareness that we are watching a film.

He is busy "deconstructing the illusion for the spectator" (West 1991, 164). When he appears as himself, we are suddenly made aware of the fact that we watch a product of the imagination. We are amused by his appearance, but experience it to some extent as an intrusion and are eager to get back to the fantasy itself. Fortunately he only stays for a few brief seconds, and we are glad to see him go. He understood fully our need to stay in touch with the illusion. He is like the analyst at the beginning and at the end of the hour and when he intervenes as a real person in his movements, sounds, interpretations, and interventions, reality intrudes. In a word, the unbridled imagination is contained. In all probability, the five-year-old Alfred, who, after his release from the jail soon surmounted his anxiety and understood that the jail sentence was a fantasy. Or was it? Was he punished or the butt of a practical joke? In either case, it would be fascinating to do unto others what had been done to him.

REFERENCES

Freud, S. 1910. A special type of choice of object made by men (Contribution to the psychology of love). *Standard Edition* 11:165–75. London: Hogarth Press.

———. 1915. The unconscious. *Standard Edition* 14:219–56. London: Hogarth Press.

———. 1919. The "uncanny." *Standard Edition* 17. London: Hogarth Press.

Hoffer, A. 1991. The Freud-Ferenczi controversy: A living legacy. *Int. Rev. Psychoanal.* 18:465–72.

Laplanche, J., and J.-B Pontalis. 1973. *The Language of Psychoanalysis.* New York: W. W. Norton.

Mulvey, L. 1989. *Visual and Other Pleasures.* Bloomington: Indiana University Press.

Raubicheck, W., and W. Srebnick 1991. *Hitchcock's Rereleased Films.* Detroit: Wayne State University Press.

Segal, H. 1991. *Dream, Phantasy, and Art*. London: Tavistock/Routledge.

Spoto, D. 1983. *The Dark Side of Genius: The Life of Alfred Hitchcock*. Boston: Little, Brown.

Taylor, S. 1991. A talk by Samuel Taylor. In Raubicheck and Srebnick 1991, 288–99.

Tomlinson, D. 1991. "They should be treated like cattle": Hitchcock and the question of performance. In Raubicheck and Srebnick 1991, 95–108.

Truffaut, F. 1983. *Hitchcock*. Rev. ed. New York: Simon and Schuster.

Trumpener, K. 1991. Fragments of the mirror: Self-reference, mise-en-abyme, *Vertigo*. In Raubicheck and Srebnick 1991, 175–88.

West, A. 1991. The concept of the fantastic in *Vertigo*. In Raubicheck and Srebnick, 1991, 163–74.

Nine

8 1/2

AND THE DISINHIBITION

of Creativity

There is a significant psychological shift from the character of Scottie Ferguson in Hitchcock's *Vertigo* (see chapter 8) to that of Guido Anselmi in Federico Fellini's *8 1/2*. Hitchcock presented us with a vision of a man who is essentially lost, at the end of his career, disabled by the effects of a devastating symptom, and incapacitated by fears over which he had no control. His only recourse was an attempt at cure through an alliance with another vulnerable and appropriated soul who was similarly afflicted. By becoming preoccupied with Madeleine, Scottie could overcome his isolation, and in bringing her back to reality, he would enable himself to travel the same route. When these plans went awry and he found himself repeating a situation in which he found himself again responsible for the death of another person by a fall which he could not prevent, he was rendered totally helpless. His only recourse then was to bring back the dead and recreate the person whom he had lost in fantasy. After having done so successfully, he could unmask the deception, overcome his inhibition, and emerge asymptomatic.

Guido Anselmi is also a deeply troubled man but unlike Scottie, he does not suffer from neurotic symptomology. Guido's task is to overcome a paralyzing block in his artistic creativity.

Metz has succinctly written that *8½* "is a powerful creative meditation on the inability to create" (1974, 234), thus quite rightly identifying the central theme of this film. The film is regarded as Fellini's masterpiece, a work which comes in the midpoint in his career and marks a critical transition and a stylistic shift from neo-realism to the incorporation of the imaginative fantasy of his later work.

THE NARRATIVE

Although *8½* plays havoc with our usual conception of classical narrative, it provides the scaffolding of a plot and structure. Guido, a forty-three-year-old movie director of films previously "lacking in hope," awakes from a nightmare at a water spa where he is taking the cure. In his nightmare, he is trapped in his car in an underpass where the traffic has come to a standstill. Other drivers in other cars, similarly stalled, look at him impassively or indifferently. In fact, in one such car, he notes a woman, whom we later learn is his mistress, being fondled by a man. Titillated by the seduction, Guido becomes intensely anxious. Claustrophobic, he desperately tries to claw his way out of his car; eventually he manages to fly into the air above. He is brought down by a man far below him, who pulls him down by a rope tied to his ankle.

The doctors prescribe a week of rest and hydrotherapy. Guido is soon joined by his collaborative script writer, Daumier, an intellectual and hostile critic who has been reading a prospective script, and he finds much to criticize in a movie Guido is about to make.

As Guido emerges from his bedroom into the bathroom, we note he is haggard, his eyes are baggy, and his cheeks are hollow. When he enters the grounds of the spa, we note that the vast and orderly line of people queuing up for their mineral water are

9.1 Federico Fellini's *8½*. Courtesy of The Museum of Modern Art/Film Stills Archive.

well dressed in costumes of the 1930s—although the movie is meant to have the contemporary setting of the early 1960s. As Guido is about to receive his glass of water, he has a vision of a beautiful woman, Claudia, dressed in a white uniform, who hands it to him. The vision of Claudia replaces the impatient and overheated attendant, whom we soon see is the dispenser in reality. Claudia appears several times during the course of the film in a variety of roles; at this point, she is the embodiment of a radiant Ideal. Soon Guido meets a friend, Mezzabotta, a guest at the spa, a middle-aged man who has taken up with a young mistress. Guido departs for the train station to greet his mistress,

Carla, whom he has invited to be present with him at the spa. She is a bird-brain, earthy and sensual, and as they make love that night, she urges Guido to find a job for her husband. Guido, as part of their foreplay, asks her to pretend she is a whore.

When he falls asleep, he dreams of his parents, who are dead. His father complains about the smallness of his grave. In the dream, his parents are disappointed in him, in that he has not achieved more. His elderly mother turns into his wife, and kisses him passionately. The next day, Guido appears at the hotel spa, and he is confronted by his producer, actresses, technicians, and many others who are expecting to work on the film with him; he is very uncertain about the nature of the film. Producers are concerned about the cost, actresses about parts that they will play. A number of hangers-on, such as journalists and tourists, press him for information, but he is preoccupied and parries their enquiries.

That evening, there is dancing on the terrace at the spa. A magician, Maurice, works with a telepathist, Maya, who reads the minds of the people who attend. Maurice uncovers that Guido is thinking of nonsense syllables, "Asa Nisi Masa."

The scene then shifts to a memory of Guido's childhood. Guido is a small boy of about eight being put to bed by a young woman, perhaps a nanny, in a very tender and supportive setting. He sleeps in a room with a number of other children, and when his grandmother leaves the room, he is told by an older girl that if one repeats the magical formula, "Asa Nisi Masa," then the eyes in a portrait that hangs on the wall will begin to move and direct its gaze to a treasure in the room.[1] When Guido awakes from his

---

1. "Asa Nisi Masa" is a phrase in which "sa" or "si" are added to a vowel in a word, much as in pig Latin. Thus, the phrase stands for "anima," "soul," or "spirit" in Italian. Commentators who have been impressed by Fellini's interest in Jung have commented that "anima" in Jungian psychology stands for the feminine part of the masculine personality as well as "spirit" or "soul," and is

memories of his childhood, he is pressured in the lobby of the hotel by an aging French actress who wants to know about her part in the film, but he is unable to tell her. On the phone, he invites his wife, Luisa, to come stay with him at the spa. He then enters a room which has been turned into a production office at the spa hotel, where his crew is busily engaged in planning the film. He is plagued by their demands on him, and when he enters his own room, he has another fantasy of Claudia, who appears as a symbol of purity and innocence. She promises that she will never leave him and will help him make order out of the mess of his life. The fantasy is interrupted when his mistress, Carla, who is staying at another hotel, calls to say that she is ill, and he rushes over to take care of her.

The next day, he is eager to have an audience with a cardinal, who is also a patient at the spa. The meeting with the elderly cardinal recalls for him another event of his childhood, when he and a group of boys ran off from the Catholic school that they were attending to visit Saraghina, a huge woman who lived by herself on the beach. They paid her to dance provocatively for them. They are apprehended by priests from the school, who reprimand them severely, telling them that Saraghina is the devil to be avoided. However, in spite of his punishment, the next day Guido returns to see her again.

Returning to the present, while in the steam baths at the hotel, Guido is again summoned by the cardinal for an audience, and is told that there is no salvation outside of the church. Shortly there-

---

understood as being a foundation for one's creativity (Burke 1986). There has been some question about whether Fellini was in Jungian psychoanalysis prior to the making of 8½. Alpert (1986) stated in his biography that Fellini had told him he had not had an analysis. However, he had read a good deal about Jung, and found his thought more compatible than the thought of Freud. Freud, said Fellini (1983), makes you think. Jung, on the other hand, was a better traveling companion for someone who wanted to find out about himself, the assumption being *by* himself. More on Jung, below.

after, his wife arrives. Initially, they have a friendly exchange, but we learn later that the wife has seen his mistress in the town, and she turns distant and cold toward him. Guido and his wife's friends visit a set that has been built for the film that he is about to make. The set consists of a launching tower for a space ship, since the original plan for the film was to be a science fiction account of people who are leaving the earth in order to live on another planet. Guido is continuously harangued by his author-critic, Daumier, and his producer, Pace, as well as by his wife, and Luisa's friends, who tell him that he has "nothing to say."

That night Luisa and Guido do not share a bed. She accuses him of deceit, and he dissimulates, claiming that he did not know that his mistress was present. The next day, when Guido and his wife are sitting at a cafe, Carla arrives, dressed in a flamboyant and exhibitionistic manner, in contrast to his sedate and conservative wife. Guido continues to lie about his knowledge of Carla's presence, denying he had invited her.

The film then depicts a fantasy which takes place in the childhood setting of the farmhouse, in which he as an adult now has a harem. He is initially in full control of all of the women in his life: his mistress, his wife, the demanding actresses, and other women with whom he had been involved earlier. He even has the capacity to ban them when they become too old—over twenty six. However, the fantasy collapses, and it ends on a depressive note in which it becomes clear to him that he had tried to turn his wife into his servant.

The mise-en-scène then shifts to the auditorium of a movie theater, and we witness the screen tests for the movie that Guido is planning to make. The producer, the producer's technicians, the writer, Guido's wife and her friends, and Guido himself are all present. The screen tests are for characters who will play parts in Guido's life, such as his mistress and his wife. Guido is very distressed, and he is unable to choose who will perform.

His wife, who sits in the audience watches herself being depicted unsympathetically and departs in anger, shouting that he is incapable of love and tells him to go to hell. Claudia appears now in reality, with the expectation that she will be an actress in his play. However, when Claudia and Guido drive off to talk about the play and her role, his indecision proves disappointing to her as well, and she also tells him several times he has no capacity for love. He resolves that he will give up the film, but the producer and his entourage find him and tell him there will be a press conference the next day. Guido reluctantly arrives for the press conference, and he is bombarded with questions about the film that he cannot answer. In desperation, he hides under the table, and has a fantasy that he commits suicide.

However, in actuality, he adheres to his decision to give up on the film. And as the set is being dismantled, Daumier, the discouraging critic, tells him he has made the wisest choice since the film would have been a failure; since he has nothing to say, and it is best to be silent. At this nadir, Maurice, the magician, appears to tell him that they are ready to begin. Guido has an overwhelming sense of joy and strength, and realizes that his despair was unjustified. It is important for him now to accept himself as he is and to accept the people in his life as they are, and everyone reappears, dressed in white, except Claudia, the Ideal, and the dissuading Daumier. They form a circle, Guido and his wife join, and the film ends with Guido as a small boy playing a fife, accompanied by circus clowns, who then depart. Guido remains alone in the middle of the circle, playing his fife. When he disappears, we are left in darkness until we see the list of credits, after which appears "Fine."

PREVIOUS VIEWS OF 8½

A film as rich in content as 8½ can readily yield itself to a variety of critical interpretations, and commentators have often noted the connection with the theme of creativity.[2] In addition, many have found the film significant as a spiritual quest. Lewalski ([1964] 1978) has pointed out the similarity in Guido's journey to that of Dante's in *Purgatorio*. The film emphasizes the need to make order out of chaos, to settle on an absolute predominance of one element over another, and the resultant conflict in trying to make a film in the absence of an overriding and consistent philosophical position. Hyman (1978) has also explored the theme of spirituality, pointing out how Guido is drawn to the Church but finds it inadequate. Guido substitutes for an integrated philosophical stance the experience of synthesizing his spiritual needs within the context of cinematic form. He cannot exclude his bad conscience as represented by Daumier, in fact he needs him as a focus for projection. It is only close to the end that Daumier is hanged in fantasy. As Guido needs Daumier, he also needs his Catholic background, which provides him with a structure against which he may test his own boundaries (Rosenthal 1976).

Others also have examined the various stations through which Guido's purgatorial journey takes place. Claudia, as the Ideal, the Virgil-like accompanist, is given up. Maurice, the clown-magician who introduces Guido to himself as a child, is a better guide to the vitalizing source for which he seeks (Costello 1981, 1983). Conti and McCormack (1984) point out that aging as a metaphor of deterioration is related to the theme of creativity. The elderly guests of the spa, the desperate attempt of Guido's friend, Mezzabotta, to renew his youth with his beautiful young mistress, the aging of the senile cardinal to whom Guido turns for futile help—all express the drying up of creative energies and the nearness of death. Branigan (1984) has emphasized how the theme of dying is transcended in the final ending, as art becomes the ultimate achieve-

2. MacDonald (1969), as well as the aforementioned Metz (1974), stated that the film is a masterpiece dealing with someone trying to break through his creative block. Branigan (1984) stated that the film explores the sources for creative impotence.

ment, the order through which chaos is conquered. Bachman (1985) points out the importance of the role of women in the film and finds support in Fellini's comment, "You project upon [a woman] what you are waiting to reveal to yourself" (26). Affron ([1990] 1993) commented on the spatial arrangements of the film, pointing out the sense of claustrophobic confinement at the beginning, the unpredictable angles from which the film is shot, the spotlighting at the end that accentuates the centrality of the child. Bondanella (1992) has dealt at length with the manner in which the film highlights the preoccupation with filmmaking as an activity and the manner by which fantasy is revealed, how Fellini avoided establishing shots, speeding up the sequence, and the utilization of the lighting and sounds of a studio sound stage in the actual content of the film itself.

THE BLENDING OF FANTASY, DREAM, MEMORY, AND REALITY

In attempting a description of the narrative in *8½*, one is hard-pressed to present a chronological account. It is only in retrospect that one becomes aware of the import of sequences and segments as they are depicted. The film opens in silence, with a view of the back of a man's head, sitting in a car, stuck in a huge traffic jam in a tunnel. There is nothing to indicate that we are visualizing a dream taking place in the mind of the protagonist, whom we do not see frontally until more than thirty shots later.[3]

When we examine the form of *8½* as it is optically articulated,

3. The scripts for *8½* have been published by Rutgers University Press (Affron 1987), and thus we have an opportunity to see the inconsistencies between the original shooting script and the continuity script and also note how non-narrative components of the film often intrude. For example, when Guido first sees himself in the bathroom after his examination by the doctors at the spa, we are confronted by a sudden upsurge of bright lights and a buzzer sound, both of which remind us that we are in the presence of a movie sound stage (shot 33).

we find ourselves perplexed by the variety of psychological phenomena with which we are presented. Since there is no establishing shot at the beginning of the film to indicate where we are, there is little to indicate that we are inside the head of the man whose back we see. Similarly, we are not quite clear when Claudia appears at the water fountain that she is not real until she is displaced by the impatient attendant. We accept that the childhood scene at the farmhouse and visit to Saraghina are visualizations of memories. However, in the confessional that follows the Saraghina episode, the booths are distorted and our own placement is disrupted so that we are left spatially disoriented. By the time Claudia appears at the screening, we are doubtful of her reality because we have seen her previously as only a figment of Guido's imagination. The reconciliation between Luisa, the wife, and Carla, the mistress, is so bizarre and contrary to our expectation, yet there is no prodromal shot such as a closeup of Guido to indicate that a fantasy is forming in his head. In the final reconciliation scene, fantasy and reality are so thoroughly blended there is no narrative imperative to account for the appearance of the characters in purified white, their deployment in a circle, the reconciliation between Luisa and Guido, the appearance of his parents, and Guido's pledge to accept himself. Even the appearance of Guido as a child, with his fife at the very end, is unaccounted for as a part of a sequential narrative, and thus reflects the return of the creative child.

To the extent that artistic creation is heavily dependent on a synthesizing conflation of reality, memory, dream, and fantasy, 8½ is a brilliant depiction of this interweaving. A close analysis of the film enables us to tease apart the variety of psychological phenomena. Freud (1908) has described how the formation of fantasy occurs in response to the frustrations in the life of the adult. The return to an experience of longed-for satisfaction is a remnant of the play of childhood. Insofar as the initial dream sequence in *8½* is a reflection of Guido's current life, it is a self-state dream, a sign of a threat to the dissolution of the self, which culminates in a wish to rise above his current impasse (Kohut 1977). But he cannot sustain his ascent and he is brought down to earth, to which he remains ambivalently tied. The nightmare thus sets the stage for the secure and playful memory of his childhood. In his childhood, there is a belief in a magical solution and a wish that a "roving eye"—such as that needed by an adult film director—will find a treasure in the corner of a room. Thus, the initial childhood scene is the response of an imaginative optical search to satisfy the adult lack.

An important principal guiding light in Guido's search is a continuing invocation of a magical solution. The return to the childhood memory is a regressive return to a time in his own life when a magical belief in omnipotence of thought was still possible. It is a longing instigated by the appearance of Maurice, the magician, an old friend of Guido's, who himself does not know how his accomplice, Maya, is able to carry out her magical telepathic tricks. Guido comments to Maurice, "We haven't seen each other for years" (Affron 1987, 81, shot 219). Maurice is the instigator who connects Guido with his past, thus bringing back that period in his life characterized by narcissistic omnipotence.

The vicissitudes of creativity are deployed through the narcissistic aspects of the personality of Guido, who is presented to us as deeply flawed. Although his primary task is to overcome the inhibition and doubt that block his creativity and this blockage is presented as "a creative illness" (Ellenberger 1970), there are emphatic statements throughout of his narcissistic vulnerability. He is repeatedly told that he is incapable of forming a loving attachment to anyone. Although he is presented in a setting in which medical treatment and a prescription by physicians is part of the milieu, he is not in a hospital, and the spa venue is blended with upper-class frivolity and luxury. Guido is incapable of object constancy, and has apparently effected a separation in his love life between the whore-like propensities of his mistress and the rigidities of his wife. He lies to both, and as much as he can, tries to avoid responsibility by flight. The split in his sexuality is suggested by the ready connection that he establishes between his mother and wife. He turns to his father, but he feels that he has received little from his father, and he has given little to him in return. At the same time, he has a deep sense of unconscious guilt, and he seeks absolution and direction through the hands of religious authority, an authority that he cannot however trust. Thus, the Church provides no source of spiritual guidance. His fantasies consist of grandiose wishes to obtain mastery and dominance, particularly over women, and to see himself as an indulgent authority whom they must obey, as in the harem sequence. While wishing to maintain a position of dominance and mastery with regard to the feminine figures in his life, Guido sees men primarily as being inadequate objects of idealization. It is no wonder that he turns to his storehouse of memories and a transformation of these memories by means of elaborated fantasy.

The first break in the narrative sequence is presented in the memory of the childhood kitchen scene, the most direct return to a nonambivalent, preoedipal stage of nurturance and care, unbounded by the constraints of reality. When Guido awakens from this fantasy and is immediately confronted by the demands of the production office, in order to escape he then envisages the image of Claudia, who offers the healing water and is also the woman who loves him, who shares his bed, and who provides him with the satisfaction for all his needs.

From the fantasy of Claudia, we return to the reality of his mistress, Carla's illness, and the hope that the church may provide him with the spiritual support that he needs. However, the church is tied associatively to the memory of Saraghina, the beginning of sexual interest, and the punishment which he received by the fathers for his misdemeanor. Although the Saraghina episode is presented as a memory rather than a fantasy, we witness the distortion added by the intervening years in the confusion about the size and position of the confessional boxes. Guido, in returning to Saraghina, establishes that he cannot live without sexuality as an important force in his life.

The meeting between Guido, his wife, and Carla in the open air cafe then serves as a day residue for the harem fantasy. The harem fantasy in itself is a compromise between Guido now as an adult, with all of the women in his adult life, and Guido who is obeyed, indulged, and catered to as a child. In fact, the restriction on women who are beyond the age of twenty six continues the notion of the importance of youthfulness which the forty-three-year-old man tries to sustain. However, already within the harem fantasy, he recognizes the impossibility of its continuance and its inevitable lack of success. The women are dissatisfied, and although he is treated as a child-king, his control is fragile and the last episode has a strong depressive ring.

The next sequence of the screen tests are given a heightened sense of reality. Of the several women who try out for roles as figures in his life, none of the women proves satisfactory. Guido makes another effort to escape from frustration in reality after his wife abandons him. He turns to Claudia as a final attempt to reach out to an Ideal. But Claudia turns out to be just another actress, interested in her role as other actresses are, equally confronting and critical of his narcissistic preoccupations.

By the time of the press conference at the site for the spaceship, Guido is bereft of his compensatory resources. He has been abandoned by his Ideal, he cannot respond to the accusatory demands; indeed, he feels that he has nothing to offer. As viewers, we are not clear at what point the reality gives way to the fantasy. There is no dissolve to inform us that in reality he is not told that there is a revolver in his pocket and that the attempt at suicide is a fantasy. Although once again we leave the realm of reality to find a solution in fantasy, this time the solution is an admission of total failure.

We return to reality with the dismantlement of the spaceship set and the reappearance of Maurice, and the last few minutes of the film are a visualization of the resolution by means of internal fantasy. He imagines that the figures of his life are all dressed in white, they form a circle around him, and everyone participates in the dance. Perhaps the only moment of actuality is the partial conciliation with his wife. Lastly, he envisages himself as a young boy playing the fife, and the film ends with a heightened return to a new reality, the reality of the theatrical spotlight, the darkened theater, the list of collaborators, and the credits, which precede the notice that the film is over.

The end of the film leaves us with little in the way of hope for the resolution of Guido's personality difficulties. He does not come to a resolution as far as his sexuality is concerned, but continues to maintain ties to both his mistress and his wife. Earlier we noted that in his dream, his mother kisses him sensually on the lips, and then becomes his wife, Luisa, an indication of his incapacity for object differentiation and a sign of condemnation for his adultery. There is little to suggest the type of working through we generally attribute to someone who has undergone a successful conflict resolution as a result of insight.

Throughout the film we have moved back and forth between actual events and mental responses to these events. These mental responses, whether in the forms of percepts, memories, images, dreams, or fantasies, have been presented through visualizations, which occupy varying time frames. Guido observes himself actively responding with an array of inner representations which he will subsequently organize into the subject of his film.

ENDOPSYCHIC PERCEPTION

Confronted with the enigma of the creative activity of the artist, as we know, Freud tended to throw up his hands.[4] When we are confronted with a masterpiece like Fellini's *8½*, however, we have an opportunity to observe the process of creativity in the process of disinhibition. Both through the mind of Guido and the contribution of his creator, Fellini, a number of critical psychological processes are depicted in *statu nascendi*. *8½* offers an example of the shift that takes place from states of psychological conflict and inhibition, to creative work. Insofar as this is the case, the film exploits the belief that there is an inverse relationship between psychological dysfunction and creative activity. Freud noted the similarity between hysterical fantasies and the mechanism of creative writing (Freud 1887–1902, 208). Not only is the creative activity a derivative of childhood play, but it is also a blending of fantasy, memory, and dream in the form of organized ego functions, the purpose of which can be devoted to the resolution of aesthetic problems.

The final circular dance is a wishful representation of the transformation and the capacity of the ego to rework defensive

---

4. Compare his well-known disclaimer on the inaccessibility of the artistic function, "The nature of the artistic function is . . . inaccessible to us along psychoanalytic lines" (Freud 1910, 136). "Before the problem of the creative artist analysis must, alas, lay down its arms" (Freud 1928, 177). "Investigations of this kind [works like M. Bonaparte's *The Life and Work of Edgar Allen Poe: A Psychoanalytic Interpretation*]. . . . are not intended to explain an author's genius, but they show what motive forces aroused it and what material was offered to him by destiny" (Freud 1933).

and avoidance mechanisms via sublimation.[5] Of critical importance in a work like *8½* is the presence of such a wide variety of
mental contents in the form of fantasy throughout the continuity
of the entire work. Members of the audience who are profoundly
moved by the ending only in retrospect realize that it in itself is
a fantasy, presumably in the mind of Guido, and its magical
quality has little to do with the likely execution or completion of
his wish to make a successful film. We respond to the notion that
he experiences joy because he now feels disinhibited; he can
make the film we are witnessing.

An essential component of Guido's creativity is his capacity to
utilize the varieties of his experience in the preparation of this
film. The film he is now about to make is a reversal of the
original film, an assumed science fiction journey to another
planet which would be an escape from the experience of his own
life. However, long before the film that we witness has come to
an end, the screen tests reveal to us that he is already preparing
to use his own experience as part of the film. Actresses portray
his wife and mistress, and are given direction about how they
are to dress and talk and act; they are to be like the figures in the
portions of the film we have already seen. Carla in fact wears the
same dress, and Luisa the same glasses. Guido's doubts during
the screen tests and his verbal commands in the tests themselves

---

5. Ariel's words from *The Tempest:*

> Full fathom five my father lies;
>   Of his bones are coral made;
> Those are pearls that were his eyes:
>   Nothing of him that doth fade,
> But thus suffer a sea-change
>   Into something rich and strange.

make an excellent poetic statement for the transforming process. They are particularly apt when we consider the cemetery scene of Guido's father's grave and the
frequent references to water and bathing which pervade many of the segments
of *8½.*

are an indication of his dissatisfaction with the performances and his inability to make a choice among the actresses.

We are left to assume that Guido, with time, realizes that subjectivity, the collation of the mental contents which pervade his mind, is to be his film. His task is the job of avoiding censorship of these contents and recognizing them as innovative subject matter. When the doctor initially confronts Guido with the question of whether he is to embark on another film "without hope," we assume that Guido, coming from the neorealist tradition, has recently made a film like *La Dolce Vita*. He is now to embark on a totally different genre, imaginative and fantastic elements will intrude into the narrative, and these intrusions will be heralded by the magician, Maurice. For Guido, the essential step is "to accept himself as he is and not as he would like to be." He realizes that the conditions of his work entail a sense of self-acceptance combined with a feeling of buoyancy and enthusiasm. The creative potential has been generated.

FELLINI

Many who have commented on the film have remarked on the close relationship between Fellini and the character he has created (Affron 1987; Alpert 1986; Conti and McCormack 1984; Costello 1983). Mastroianni is costumed to resemble Fellini, and Guido is forty three, the age of Fellini at the time he made the film. There are many other references to the actuality of Fellini's life. Many of the members of the technical staff who worked on the film and who appear in the final scene keep their own names. And, of course, the film is about a director who is making a film, and the film which is being made is about a film that we are seeing. As Metz (1974) points out, we are confronted with a double mirror which reflects on itself.

Shortly after the completion of *La Dolce Vita*, by October of 1960, Fellini had the outline of the *8½* story. It is striking how early he had already conceived the theme. In a letter to his friend, Brunello Rondi, he detailed the story of a man who is caught up in an infinite number of relationships and feels anchorless and emptied of resolve. The protagonist is with a wife and mistress at a spa where he is taking the water cure, and he dreams of his mother and father, who are dead. He imagines that Claudia—the actress, Claudia Cardinale—will offer him "the solution to everything" (Affron 1987, 229). Fellini saw the Saraghina episode as depicting "a horrible and splendid dragon, who represents the first traumatic view of sex in the life of the hero" (Affron 1987, 233). Fellini ended his letter to Rondi with the statement, "I realized that reflecting . . . is not useful. If I force myself to concentrate on this subject, I run the risk of completely muddling my thoughts. That's why I peacefully wait for something or someone to make me take a step forward" (Affron 1987, 234).

The letter was completed about a year and a half before the shooting of the film began, and already shows signs of an autobiographical nature. Fellini himself had spent some time at a spa in the summer of 1960. "I went for a rest cure, at a moment when things were at a low ebb. I was in limbo taking stock of myself. I needed to reconcile my fears. I asked myself the usual questions; 'Who am I? What am I doing? Where am I going?' " (Alpert 1986, 154).

Fellini had not yet decided to make his protagonist a film director, and it was only gradually that the hero took on aspects of his own personality and became an obvious surrogate. As mentioned above, there is some doubt as to whether Fellini had some Jungian analysis prior to the making of 8½, and although in 1984 he denied to his biographer, Alpert, that he had been in analysis, he had had some contact with a Dr. Ernest Bernhard, a Jungian analyst whom he had met as a result of a parapraxis. One day he was dialing the phone number of a woman in whom he was interested, and found that he had dialed the name of the analyst instead. When the man answered the phone and identified himself as

Bernhard, Fellini said he was trying to reach the number of a beautiful lady. The analyst said, "I'm sorry, but I'm an old man" (Alpert 1986, 169). Magically, Fellini had found his treasure. He arranged to meet with him, and they subsequently became good friends. Later he stated that Dr. Bernhard explained his thoughts to him, presented him with a new way of looking at life, and making use of experiences and energies buried under rubbles of fears and neglected wounds (170). Thus, however ambiguous Fellini's experience with Jung may have been, the contact with Jungian psychology proved salutary. Jung freed him "from the sense of guilt and inferiority complex" (177) with which a constraining and systematic philosophical position had left him. As a film maker, he moved from a neorealistic position to one in which imaginative and nonrealistic forms of cinema were preferred, and he could identify himself more readily as the protagonist of his own film. He stated, "self-acceptance can occur only when you've grasped that the only thing that exists is yourself, your true, deep self which wants to grow spontaneously, but which is fettered by inoperative lies, and myths and fantasies that propose an unattainable morality or sanctity or perfection—all of it brain-washed into us during our defensive childhood" (178). Fellini's comments emphasize a turning to a view of an expanded self which finds the diversity of the subjective world as sources for creativity (Greenacre 1957, 1958; Kohut 1977).

It is generally believed that the title of the film is outside the diegesis. It has little to do with the content and is a reflection of the position of the film in the oeuvre of the director.[6] Perhaps this is not altogether true, particularly if we consider the promi-

6. Fellini himself claimed that the title is nondiegetic, a reference to his seven full-length films and two shorts. Baxter (1994, 189) suggests some additional meanings for the title 8½. He points out that in an interview he had been informed that Fellini had had his first sexual experience when he was eight and a half, that if one counts Carla as a half-share, women in the farmhouse harem

nence with which Fellini presents the latency-aged child at the end. This is the child who can still believe in magic, who with his fife is still able to serve as the leader of the motley band of circus performers, the child at the verge of losing some of the richness of imaginative fantasies and to whom the director must return in order to disinhibit his own creativity.

SUMMARY

The achievement of *8½* lies in Fellini having privileged the subjectivity of intrapsychic experience as an aspect of creativity. Fellini was able to surmount the barriers which neorealism had left him from his earlier films and turn to imaginative forms whereby fantasy would be juxtaposed within narrative contexts. The film emphasizes that endopsychic perception can serve as a useful source for the creative artistic impulse. Such forms of presentation depend on the utilization of the imaginative capacities of childhood, which are to be recathected, disinhibited, given free rein, and not allowed to be extinguished by the demands of confining reality.

REFERENCES

Affron, C. 1987. *8½: Federico Fellini, Director.* New Brunswick: Rutgers University Press.
———. [1990] 1993. Order and the space for spectacle in Fellini's *8½*. In *Perspectives on Federico Fellini,* ed. P. Bondanella and C. Degli-Esposti. New York: G. K. Hall.

---

come to eight and a half, and in addition he was informed that the Fellini children, when young, were forced to go to bed every night at 8:30! Charles Kligerman, M.D. (personal communication) has pointed out the connection with nine months of pregnancy and inhibited creativity.

Alpert, H. 1986. *Fellini: A Life*. New York: Atheneum.

Bachman, G. 1985. And the ship sails on. *Film Comment* 21 (June): 25–30.

Baxter, J. 1994. *Fellini*. New York: St. Martin's Press.

Bondanella, P. 1992. *The Cinema of Federico Fellini*. Princeton: Princeton University Press.

Branigan, E. 1984. *Point of View in the Cinema*. Berlin: Mouton Publishers.

Burke, F. 1986. Modes of narration and spiritual development in Fellini's *8½*. *Literature/Film Quarterly* 14(3):164–70.

Conti, I., and W. A. McCormack. 1984. Federico Fellini: Artist in search of self, *Biography* 7(3):292–318.

Costello, D. P. 1981. Layers of reality: *8½* as spiritual autobiography. *Notre Dame English Journal* 13(2):1–12.

———. 1983. *Fellini's Road*. Notre Dame: University of Notre Dame Press.

Ellenberger, H. 1970. *The Discovery of the Unconscious*. New York: Basic Books.

Fellini, F. [1960] 1987. Letter to Brunello Rondi, October 1960. In *8½: Federico Fellini, Director*, ed. C. Affron. New Brunswick: Rutgers University Press.

———. 1983. *Comments on Film*. Ed. G. Grazzini. Fresno: The Press at California State University.

Freud, S. 1887–1902. *The Origins of Psychoanalysis*. Ed. M. Bonaparte, A. Freud, and E. Kris. New York: Basic Books.

———. 1908. Creative writers and day-dreaming. *Standard Edition* 9:143–53. London: Hogarth Press.

———. 1910. Leonardo da Vinci and a memory of his childhood. *Standard Edition* 11:63–137. London: Hogarth Press.

———. 1928. Dostoevsky and parricide. *Standard Edition* 21:177–94. London: Hogarth Press

———. 1933. Preface to Marie Bonaparte's *The Life and Works of Edgar A. Poe: A Psychoanalytic Interpretation*. *Standard Edition* 22:254. London: Hogarth Press.

Greenacre, P. 1957. The childhood of the artist: Libidinal phase development and giftedness. *Psychoanalytic Study of the Child* 12:47–72.

———. 1958. The family romance of the artist. *Psychoanalytic Study of the Child* 13:9–36.

Hyman, T. 1978. *8½* as an anatomy of melancholy. In *Federico Fellini. Essays in Criticism*, ed. P. Bondanella. New York: Oxford University Press. 121–29.

Kohut, H. 1977. *The Restoration of the Self.* New York: International Universities Press.

Lewalski, B. K. [1964] 1978. Federico Fellini's Purgatorio. In *Federico Fellini: Essays in Criticism,* ed. P. Bondanella. Bloomington: Indiana University Press.

MacDonald, D. 1969. *Dwight MacDonald on Movies.* Englewood Cliffs, N.J.: Prentice Hall.

Metz, C. 1974. *Film Language: A Semiotics of the Cinema.* New York: Oxford University Press.

Rosenthal, S. 1976. *The Cinema of Federico Fellini.* Cranburg, NJ: A. S. Barnes.

Trosman, H. 1985. *Freud and the Imaginative World.* Hillsdale, N.J.: The Analytic Press.

{ *Ten* }

PSYCHOANALYTIC
ATTRIBUTES
of Quality in Art

*A study that essays a contemporary psychoanalytic approach to out-*standing works in the visual arts and film necessitates a continu-ing confrontation—begun in chapter 2—with what we mean by "masterpiece" or "quality." We live in an age which does not take kindly to the concept of masterpiece. Our current era has emphasized multiculturalism and highlighted the fact that much of the Western tradition has excluded valuable Eastern and Afri-can contributions, and American and European culture generally has been characterized as limited by a restricted immersion in the work of dead white males. Some consider that the notion of masterpiece is an expression of commodification, an ideological mask for the preservation of an established order.

A recent attempt by Bloom (1994) in *The Western Canon* has been considered an atavistic retreat from a more enlightened position, a vain and futile attempt that has met with serious criticism (Adams 1994; McGrath 1994; Donoghue 1995). Bloom has based the canon largely around the figure of Shakespeare, thus establishing the dramatist as a standard by which to mea-sure the value of others. In subscribing to the view that a single figure is the touchstone, limitations of method arise. A field as complex as Western literature does not lend itself easily to the application of a single standard of greatness. Canons shift with time, and a work which may be highly valued in one era may be found wanting in another. A new epoch may discern richness in a neglected master. Adams points out that shortly after its appearance, James Joyce's *Ulysses* was described by an authoritative canonizer as "an explosion in a sewer" (Adams 1994, 6). History warns us of the danger of canonizing, and Bloom's views have been attacked as lacking in cogency of argumentation, guilty of bias, manifestly exclusionary, arbitrary, and excessively bound to a sense of literary tradition.

The approach in this book has not been to establish a canon, either in the realm of painting or of film. I am inclined to accept that there is a consensus about a dozen or so masters in each category; in the visual arts, there is general agreement about the status of Leonardo da Vinci, Raphael, Michelangelo, Giorgione, Titian, Poussin, Velázquez, Rembrandt, Tiepolo, Goya, Manet, Seurat, Cézanne, and Picasso, and among filmmakers, Griffith, Eisenstein, Vigo, Renoir, Welles, Bergman, Fellini, Hitchcock, Antonioni, Ford, Godard, Truffaut, and Kurosawa.

For some, perhaps even such a list is likely to lead to dissension. One or more who are listed are not eligible and many more who are not named should be. Some may indeed believe that the whole issue, as mentioned heretofore by the critics of Bloom, is a nonissue and that so much subjectivity and convention are associated with such lists that the task is futile. In any case, I believe the issue of who is in and who is out is of less importance for my purpose than a careful analysis of selected works in order to demonstrate the utility of a contemporary psychoanalytic approach as a potential for the attribution of value.

What Bloom has recently attempted in literature and what others, of course, have done many times in the past has also been attempted in the visual arts and film. Rosenberg (1967), as mentioned in chapter 2, has attempted an analysis of quality in the visual arts and did a comparative analysis among drawings in order to demonstrate how a great draftsman could provide particular qualities in the tension, skill, and liveliness with which line could be applied, and such excellence could be differentiated from that of a mediocre craftsman. Gombrich (1968) found fault with such an approach, just as Adams (1994) could find fault with that of Bloom. The polls by *Sight and Sound* magazine every ten years attempt a similar estimation of excellence for film, and here too there is dissension among the skeptics. Generally such dissension is possible because the criteria of excellence are unspecified, unexamined, and attributable to subjective judgment, which is subject to taste and tradition. Few today will ascribe to a particular critic or connoisseur the qualities of a standard-setter. I propose that since psychological factors are critical in aesthetic judgment, works which are judged to be masterworks should be considered within a psychoanalytic framework.

Such an approach to works of art has entered psychoanalytic discourse. Rose (1980, 1991) has investigated the aesthetic experience in terms of psychological states of tension and release which contribute to a subjective sense of wholeness. Likierman (1989) has offered an extensive psychoanalytic approach to aesthetic experience, an analysis also based on aspects of form. Likierman traces the aesthetic to experiences of early life, and shares with Rose the view that such experiences are preconceptual and likely to be pre-ideational. Satisfaction of needs is accompanied by appreciation attached to the satisfying object. The aesthetic is given a subjective base since as an attribute of infantile omnipotence, it is difficult to conceive of an experience which is not produced by the archaic self. The infant feels that it produces its own needs and environment, and much of aesthetic value is based on formation of a restored totality in the face of frustration and potential fragmentation.

Add to this early quality of the aesthetic, learned responses that are dependent upon the development of a variety of ego capacities, including sublimation and the capacity to surmount the dissatisfactions associated with primary needs. An important component in further development of the aesthetic is the quality of strangeness and uncanniness associated with novelty and innovation (Freud 1919). Such novelty, with time, becomes characterized by familiarity, and objects have the capacity to reinvoke experience with a gradually decreasing sense of unfamiliarity.

When we extend an understanding of early experiences into the realm of judgments of art, we note that the artwork is not merely an external object but also a form of representation of a striving and expanding self. It is an essential part of aesthetic response that an individual has the capacity to reinvent an experience of increasing integration of components of an object as occurs in the process of personality integration. Freud (1908) in "Creative Writers and Day-Dreaming" suggested that the deepest pleasure derived from art relied on the satisfaction of fantasy. Unconscious fantasies that seek expression through derivatives find satisfaction through the incentive bonus which aesthetic form could produce. In addition, the drive toward satisfaction is accompanied by developments in expanding ego and organizational structures.

A major question of psychoanalytic concern has continued to be the mode of transmission by which progress is effected from satisfaction of internal need to the actual creation of the artwork itself. How is the process which is essentially an internal psychological one transformed into one which attains external representation and then has the capacity to move others toward aesthetic satisfaction? It is likely that it takes place as a result of a process of endopsychic perception in the mind of the creator. A movement toward integration in the mind of the creative artist is externalized as a sequence of perception, striving for satisfaction, displacement to surrogates, and execution. Among some creative artists, who are sufficiently introspective to be able to follow their internal processes, such phenomena have been described. A detailed description of such transformations is offered by

Henry James as he recalled them in the preface to his novel *The Spoils of Poynton* (Trosman 1990).

The stimulus for *The Spoils of Poynton* was suggested to James in the form of a casual remark at a Christmas Eve dinner party. James allowed the single idea to gestate in his mind as a day residue for a prolonged period of time until he was ready to put it in the form of a story. During the gestation period, the day residue found the opportunity to become attached to some critical psychological issues in the life of the author. The story, as it took form, expressed an unconscious fantasy of the satisfactions he could obtain through a feminine identification and simultaneously provide him with an opportunity to find aesthetic satisfaction in the creation of a central feminine character who would be his alter ego and also give the story a coherent form. James described at some length the satisfaction he felt when he recognized he had performed a successful integration which would allow him to fulfill a creative task.

Among the particular formal qualities that are attributed to great works of art, we frequently think of coherence, unity of form and content, and the capacity to relate the variety of parts to a whole. Schapiro ([1966] 1944) recognized that in works of visual art in which the subject is relegated to a subsidiary position, the relations among the formal elements become critical and a sense of unity depends on a distribution which plays with the balance between components such as shape, light, color, space, or volume. Such tendencies toward organization may be present in nascent stages as a goal rather than an attainment. As Schapiro states, "in the greatest works of all . . . incompleteness and inconsistency are evidences of the living processes of the most serious and daring art which is rarely realized fully according to a fixed plan but undergoes the contingencies of a prolonged effort" (34). Such urges toward formal organization, whether fulfilled or accompanied by the presence of content or not, reflect a wish for psychological organization in creator or in recipient, whether in reality or fantasy. In the absence of overt content, subject matter may be latent, unavailable because of lack of the capacity for symbolization, or defensive operations such as repression, which propel toward absence (Balter 1994). However, ideational content need not be a necessary component of a work. Certainly, tension and associated psychological states can be experienced in response to abstract form, leading toward the resolution of such states (Rose 1980).[1]

The outstanding works of art that have been considered in this book have not been works of pure form. I have examined works where there has been a balance between content and form and where the balance has been masterful. Although it is impossible to conceive of a work of outstanding merit in which form was insignificant, there are variations in the degree to which form plays a part. In *Las Meninas* and *The Tempest* the relationship between meaning and the manner by which it is expressed is evenly distributed. Form is given a deserved prominence as a carrier of ideational meaning in Seurat's *Un Dimanche à la Grande Jatte* and backgrounded in the analysis of Rembrandt's self-portraits. However, even in *La Grande Jatte,* the emphasis on technique to some extent conceals the degree to which thematic components are present. Pointillism as a technique implies a synthesis between elements of colors, their complementary contrasts and a resultant unity. Seurat could not help but inject some aspects of his subjective concerns, his need to find some resolution of conflict between alienation, individuation and psychological attachment.

---

1. Nonchoral music is often seen as the carrier of such formal values in that affect, repetition, and organization find expression through auditory modalities, which lack verbal content. The paintings of Jackson Pollock of the late 1940s and early 1950s are masterworks of the twentieth century, which are also relatively pure in form.

Of the films that have been discussed, there has been a similar interest in highlighting a judicious balance between form and ideational and affective content. The tipping of the balance toward social diagnosis in Antonioni's *L'avventura* may account for its temporary displacement from the film canon. Bloom (1994) suggests that our times are in retreat from ideas which threaten us. A presumed underlying concern with normative relationships and implied condemnation of object inconstancy may be anathema today.[2] Film as a medium relies on divisible crafts in technical production; in spite of intense potential for emotional impact, cinematic theory is heavily weighted in the direction of its formal means.

The works of art discussed heretofore share universal thematic interests. They are concerned with critical aspects of human experience, motives, conflict, forms of self-recognition, identity formation, strivings in the direction of mastery, the relationship between fantasy and reality, drives toward artistic creativity, relationships characterized by the emotional constellations of loving and hating, the problematics of establishing individuation within a social and historical context. It is difficult to imagine that there will come a time when such universal concerns will no longer matter, and insofar as many of these themes cover human experience today and are so sweeping, it can be assumed that the works of art under question—insofar as they deal with these themes through a provocative variety of visual modes—present us with forms of expression that are likely to be durable.

A contemporary psychoanalytic perspective enriches what has been designated as "classical" psychoanalysis, the original Freudian canon (Valenstein 1979). In practice "classical" refers to

2. Fellini's *8½*, although engaging itself with a similar theme, evacuates the condemnatory viewer as a ridiculed hostile critic, the character Daumier.

the utilization of the standard therapeutic technique with its constituents of interpretation of resistance, the analysis of the transference and reconstruction as the essential components of the therapeutic process. "Classicity" implies some basic theoretical concepts such as the central importance of unconscious intrapsychic conflict, the centrality of the oedipus complex and pregenital derivatives, the conception of the mind in terms of a structural theory, the central importance of the primary drives, the sexual and aggressive drives, and their derivatives.

With the passage of time, although there has continued to be a predominant adherence to these fundamental theoretical components of psychoanalysis, there has been a shift in psychoanalysis toward concepts which include a more expanded frame of reference. The approach to the works of art and film under consideration in this study reflect on this expanded scope and can be understood in terms of elaborations and refinements of the classical psychoanalytic foundation. Each of the artworks examined possesses dimensions which add to the classical paradigm.

Las Meninas examines the position of the observer in the understanding of psychological processes, and highlights for us the intimate link between representation and identification of subject and object in the process of self-understanding. *The Tempest* depicts the oedipal family as a generic component of object relations and centers subjective fantasy as a route toward the rendering of external reality. *Un Dimanche à la Grande Jatte,* by concentrating on the formal relations between surface and depth, examines the developmental difficulties involved in establishing a proper balance between psychological attachment and separation. The pair of Rembrandt self-portraits reflects the process of mastery and represents gradations in the struggle to overcome and resist the experience of temporary defeat which results from adversity. *L'avventura* resonates with the difficulties in sustaining object constancy under conditions when establishing attachments becomes unfavorable and anxiety-ridden. *Citizen Kane* advances the position of the conflict with the oedipal father by emphasizing the importance of maternal object loss and compensatory narcissistic components such as archaic grandiosity and a longing for displaced derivatives and surrogates which replace the original loss. In *Vertigo*, we note recent developments in the refinements of the psychoanalytic therapeutic process, with its emphasis on enactment and the construction of a mutually resonating relationship as a condition for cure. With *8½*, we note the current interest of psychoanalysis in factors which contribute to disinhibition of creativity and the utilization through endopsychic perception of fantasy, memory, and dream as components in the formation of works of art.

A psychoanalysis which pays attention to the form by which works of art are presented adds a significant dimension to our understanding of the impact of such works. A psychoanalytic view of quality considers the process whereby unconscious content is mediated in order to provide an increase in psychological understanding. Masterworks provide the material by which psychic reality becomes increasingly better known.

REFERENCES

Adams, R. M. 1994. Bloom's all-time greatest hits. *New York Review of Books* 41(19), 17 November: 3–6.

Balter, L. 1994. Why people experience art as reality: The aesthetic illusion. Paper presented at meeting of the American Psychoanalytic Association, December. New York.

Bloom, H. 1994. *The Western Canon: The Books and School of the Ages.* New York: Harcourt Brace.

Donoghue, D. 1995. The book of genius. *The Times Literary Supplement* No. 4788, 6 Jan. 3–4.

Ellenberger, H. 1970. *The Discovery of the Unconscious.* New York: Basic Books.

Freud, S. 1908. Creative writers and day-dreaming. *Standard Edition* 9:143–53. London: Hogarth Press.

———. 1914. The *Moses* of Michelangelo. *Standard Edition* 13:211–36. London: Hogarth Press.

———. 1919. The "uncanny." *Standard Edition* 17:219–256. London: Hogarth Press.

Gombrich, E. H. 1968. How do you know it's any good? *New York Review of Books*, 1 Feb.: 5–8.

Likierman, M. 1989. Clinical significance of aesthetic experience. *International Review of Psychoanalysis* 16:133–50.

McGrath, C. 1994. Loose canon. *New Yorker*, 26 Sept.: 101–6.

Rose, G. J. 1980. *The Power of Form.* New York: International Universities Press.

———. 1991. Abstract art and emotion. Expressive form and the sense of wholeness. *J. Amer. Psychoanal. Assoc.* 39:131–56.

Rosenberg, J. 1967. *On Quality in Art: Criteria for Excellence, Past and Present.* Princeton: Princeton University Press.

Schapiro, M. [1966] 1994. On perfection, coherence and unity of form and content. In *Theory and Philosophy of Art: Style in Art and Society.* New York: George Braziller.

Trosman, H. 1990. Transformations of unconscious fantasy in art. *J. Amer. Psychoanal. Assoc.* 38:47–59.

Valenstein, A. F. 1979. The concept of "classical" psychoanalysis. *J. Amer. Psychoanal. Assoc.* 27 (supplement): 113–36.

INDEX